RAMAN SUBBA ROW

RAMAN SUBBA ROW

Cricket Visionary

Raman Subba Row

Douglas Miller

foreword by Sir John Major KG CH

CHARLCOMBE BOOKS

Charlcombe Books
17 George's Road, Bath BA1 6EY
01225 335813

First published 2017

ISBN: 978 0 9568510 8 6

Printed and bound in Great Britain by
CPI Antony Rowe, Chippenham, Wilts

Contents

This book is dedicated to the

eight grandchildren of Raman and Anne

from left: Max, Thomas, Jake, Emily, Harry, Nick, Alex, Rory

Foreword

by the Rt Hon Sir John Major KG CH

Raman Subba Row is not only a remarkable cricketer, but also a remarkable administrator. Both on the field and in committee rooms, Raman was a leader – undemonstrative, but in control.

As a player, Raman was Test Class. I first saw him bat in the mid-1950s, when I was impressed by his ability to steal singles whilst other batsmen were bogged down. Raman found gaps where his fellow batsmen found fielders; it was a talent he never lost – in cricket or in life.

And there was no doubt Raman could bat. At Whitgift School, at Cambridge, at Surrey and at Northampton, he showed his class time and again, and harnessed his talent to maximum effect. Any man who averages nearly 47 runs per innings playing for England, and over 41 throughout a first-class county career, can look back with pride at his achievements. But Raman's on-field skill is only the beginning of his story.

I came to know Raman well over 30 years ago. His playing days may have been over, but he was at the height of his influence as an administrator. In the years that followed, Raman, and his wife Anne, became cherished friends, and I watched his career with interest and admiration.

Early in his post-playing career, Raman saw that commerce could rescue cricket, but only if cricket was prepared to offer commerce a reason to do so. Typically, he acted.

As a member of the Surrey Committee, and working with similarly far-sighted Surrey stalwarts, notably Bernie Coleman and Derek Newton, Raman put flesh on the proposition that "money is the root of all progress". Surrey, and later England cricket – itself so often closer to bankruptcy than riches – were to benefit from Raman's initiatives. Some of them were innovative, many very controversial, but they were necessary.

As Chairman of Surrey, Raman argued his case with firm intelligence. He had foresight: he knew where cricket needed to go, and acted with determination and guile to push through new ideas.

The first initiative at Surrey was advertising hoardings on the ground. This was followed by match sponsorship; corporate support; day/night games; and later, on a wider canvas, selling cricket to broadcasters. The game was transformed into the one we know today, and initiatives were accompanied by reform of cricket's governing bodies and the introduction of Match Referees – all changes that were once considered to be unthinkable.

In all these advances, Raman was in the vanguard – at Surrey; as a member of the MCC Committee; Chairman of the TCCB; and a Match Referee. Where Raman went, change followed. Even when he became Manager of the England Test team on a tour of India controversy followed: a famous on-field dispute laid bare the case for independent umpires. They are now common practice.

To meet Raman Subba Row is to talk to a charming, soft-spoken, often self-effacing man: but a man of intellect who weighs his words carefully and can be unyielding about the objective he seeks. Raman has the remorseless logic and inner steel to take the action that turns ideas into accomplished fact.

Raman cares about cricket – and has fought for it throughout his adult life. He has never sought publicity or recognition, but few – if any – others have contributed so much to the game as both player and innovator.

This biography by Douglas Miller is a much-needed tribute to an unsung hero. It is a story that deserves to be told.

Introduction

There was a message on my telephone answering machine: I was asked to ring Anne Subba Row. Cricket has its famous initials – P.B.H., D.C.S., M.J.K. – but it has few more distinctive or intriguing names than Subba Row. A May, Compton or Smith might claim confused identity, but hardly a Subba Row. Moreover I had met Raman a couple of times, and I happened to know his wife's name was Anne. But what could her business be? I soon found out.

Anne had met Mike Smith in the president's box at Lord's and had seen a short book written on her husband's friend and fellow England cricketer. Would it, she wondered, be possible for something similar to be written about Raman? She would love to have it for the grandchildren, she said, barely considering that the story of a man with three centuries from 13 Tests and a lifetime dedicated to the governance of the game might be of interest to a wider audience. My telephone number was passed on and soon I was recanting my claim that I had written my last book.

We arranged to meet at the Subba Row home with its magnificent view over the Old Whitgiftians' playing field and a cricket square on which Raman continued to score runs for years after he had left the first-class game and where, even today, he would be entitled to at least as valid a view on an lbw appeal as those in many a county press box. Our meeting was supposedly exploratory, but I immediately knew that I was being offered a challenge it would be a privilege to accept.

It was entirely coincidental but helpful that I had followed Raman to Trinity Hall, Cambridge just a few years after he had made his mark at Fenner's. Thereafter cricket had taken him from his native Surrey to Northants and the captaincy of that county, to two full MCC tours and on into pivotal roles within the TCCB at times of fundamental change to the structure of the game when centres of power, both domestically and on the international front, were shifting from the benign and gentlemanly into an era of hard-nosed realism. It was a career capped by acting as match referee in no fewer than 41 Tests and 119 ODIs.

Raman was a man who had known what it was to fight his corner, but he had come through it with only the warmest of feelings for those with and against whom he had played and negotiated. Friendships forged over the years had been sustained. 'Alan Davidson was sitting in your chair only last month,' he assured me, and Jackie Hendriks would be there next week. Garry Sobers had certainly sat there. Never mind John Major, when he had popped round! As his 85th birthday loomed, Raman was constricted in movement, his legs no longer enabling him to walk far from the house, while his memory, he was quick to admit, was not to be trusted.

As we chatted I soon became grateful that Raman was so acutely aware of his own difficulties in recalling details or even the context of events in his earlier life. Having tackled six books that I would term assisted biographies and spoken to countless former players as part of my research, I had become used to confusion with dates, locations and participants in trying to recall the detail of matches. It would be so if a mere club cricketer were to attempt to unravel the detail of games played 50 or more years ago. Yet often amid the confusion there will be an important strand of truth or an observation that helps paint a more complete picture. At least with Raman I would be spared the claim that personal presence at a match transcends the records enshrined in *Wisden*. I would need to tread with care, perhaps making greater use of published material, but with the assistance of Anne and a few former playing and administrative colleagues I could surely record for posterity the deeds of a man I had already been assured had been one of the great visionaries of post-war English cricket.

Douglas Miller, March 2017

1

'A boy called Subba Row'

Early life and schooling

As the crowds thronged the shops in England with Christmas just six days away, Raman Subba Row looked out across a floodlit ground in Colombo. He was a month away from his seventieth birthday and this was the last of the 119 One-Day Internationals for which he would be appointed match referee, bringing to a close a long and varied list of appointments that had come his way in the game of cricket once his first-class playing career had ended. The match he had been overseeing had been at the R Premadasa Stadium. Constructed on terrain reclaimed from swampland, it had seen its first match in 1986, when it had taken its name from the country's president of the day.

This was 2001, and as the home crowd celebrated victory for their side in the final of the LG Abans Triangular Tournament against West Indies, Raman could reflect on the changes he had seen in the game he had come to love and which had dominated his life since he had first had a bat in his hands in the early 1930s. In his formative years there had been only Test matches between cricket's leading countries, but this final game in Colombo was a one-day encounter limited to 50 overs a side. With playing hours extending into darkness, it had been played under lights with a white ball. The players and umpires had worn coloured clothing, and the outcome of the match had been decided by a new-fangled formula known as Duckworth-Lewis. Two of the countries involved in the seven-match tournament, Sri Lanka and Zimbabwe, had changed their names though, as Ceylon and Rhodesia, neither had harboured serious pretensions to Test status when Raman played the game. Now he had been in Sri Lanka to watch all seven matches in the tournament because the ICC had decreed that all such ODIs should be presided over by a referee from an independent country.

How could the young Raman have imagined where life, or more precisely cricket, was to take him, an Anglo-Indian with a curiously memorable name, as he set out in life? His surname has always been a source of fascination, though in the coastal area some 250 miles north of Madras (now Chennai) from which his Indian father hailed, the name Subbarao was quite commonly found. Raman's father, Panguluri Venkata Subbarao was born in 1896 in the village of Bapatla, now a town of some 70,000, in Guntur District, Andhra Pradesh. In 1913 he was sent by his father to Queen's College, Cork, part of what was then the National University of Ireland, to study Law. When his four-year course was completed, Panguluri found he had to wait two weeks for the boat that would take him to Bombay (now Mumbai). Spending this time in London, he met a young English girl, Doris Mildred Pinner from Chiswick. A whirlwind romance led to marriage and when Panguluri set sail for India, he took Doris with him. It was an eventful journey. The ship on which the young couple were travelling was torpedoed by the Germans and their rescue ship took them to North Africa before they eventually made their way to Madras.

In 1920 Panguluri and Doris returned from Madras to England, where they made their home, their surname having now changed to Subba Row. 'My mother said no-one would be able to pronounce rao,' Raman explains. 'So she insisted on having it changed from rao to Row.' Doris also decided that a better first name for her husband would be Roy. Panguluri, or Roy, set to work building up his practice as a barrister. It was soon thriving as he specialised in cases that came before the Judicial Committee of the Privy Council. Still widely used across the Commonwealth, though mainly by dependent territories without full political independence, as the final court of appeal, it became a source of regular business from India in the days before the establishment of India's own Supreme Court in 1950 in the wake of independence.

Raman's parents had imagined their family complete with two sons, Gordon, born in 1918, and his brother Stanley, born in 1922; but in 1929 tragedy befell the family. Gordon was killed in a bicycle accident. Raman never knew the elder of his two brothers, believing his own birth, in Streatham on 29 January 1932, to have been prompted by his parents' wish to restore the size of their family. In 1936 they moved to the Croydon area, where Raman's father bought a house in Fairfield Road, just over a mile from the home in which Raman and his wife Anne have lived since 1965. His childhood home was within easy walking distance of Raman's first school, Coombe Hill House, where he went from the age of four.

Set at the junction of Coombe Road and Park Lane, the school occupied a spacious Georgian town house with steps leading up to an imposing main entrance set between Doric columns. The walled gardens and large rooms will have commended it in 1930 to the man who was looking for a property in which to open a school, Walter Uphill. Mr Uphill paid £3,000 for the house, where he and his wife ran the school, which took children from the age of four to eleven, throughout Raman's time there. Apart from the Uphills, Raman particularly remembers a Miss Prest as the teacher who got his formal education under way. Despite the building suffering severe damage to its

Raman's father Panguluri

brickwork from a nearby bomb during the War, the school carried on until 1966, after which the building found surprising new owners in the form of the Labour Party. In May 1967 it was opened by the Prime Minister, Harold Wilson, as Ruskin House, the name by which it is known today.

Though his father never played cricket, the family were always interested in the game and Raman suspects that some of his talent for ball games may have come from his mother's side. 'My mother's mother, my grandmother, was a Miss Hutton and her family came from Pudsey in Yorkshire, so I am pretty sure I am part of the same Hutton family as Len. I told him that one day. He just looked at me blankly. "I don't believe it," he said, "I don't believe it!"' Raman's first memory of playing any form of cricket is on the lawn at Fairfield Road, where Stanley showed his young brother how to hold a bat and bowled to him. Instinctively Raman, who does almost everything else right-handed, picked up the bat as the left-hander he would always be. Even as he recalls facing his brother's gentle lobs he sweeps his right arm across his chest as he demonstrates the preference many left-hand batsmen have for allowing the right hand to take control of the bat. It is the equivalent in most racket games of favouring the backhand over the forehand, where greater use is made of the wrist.

Coombe Hill House gave Raman his first experience of playing formal cricket, for which the boys had to go up to nearby Lloyd Park. They enjoyed matches against other prep schools, and Raman was already a useful left-hand bat and right-arm spinner when he moved on to nearby Whitgift School at the age of eleven. The school has long enjoyed enviable facilities for sport which, since the turn of the century, have seen Surrey playing regular championship and List A matches on the main cricket ground. Among several former pupils in the first-class game, England One Day International Jason Roy and Matthew Spriegel are two who have returned to play for Surrey on their school ground, while Dominic Sibley, in the summer of 2013, was given leave from school to represent Surrey and became the youngest player to score a double century in the County Championship. The staging of county matches has been a particular source of satisfaction to Dr Christopher Barnett, the school's long-serving headmaster. Recalling R. Subba Row as one of his childhood heroes, he was thrilled on arrival to find Raman an active Old Whitgiftian, proudly welcoming him as a friend and special guest in the headmaster's marquee for the big matches.

At Whitgift School
Raman, Ted Dexter, Dr Christopher Barnett, Matthew Spriegel, Jason Roy

Though founded in 1596 by John Whitgift, the last Archbishop of Canterbury in the reign of Elizabeth I, the school moved as recently as 1931 to what had once been the country estate of Lord Howard of Effingham, Admiral of the Fleet at the time of the Armada. Its 45 acres of parkland include areas devoted to the encouragement of wildlife. Peacocks, dating back to the 1930s, and flamingos are among birds parading the grounds, but there is also an ever-widening provision for sport, where the Sports and Conference Centre, opened in 2005 by the Duke of York, includes a room named after Raman.

The school that Raman joined in 1943 was exclusively for day boys, though a boarding house has subsequently been opened. Like many public schools, Whitgift battled through the War relying on staff many of whom had long passed retirement age. Raman's first headmaster, too, stayed longer than he otherwise might. Gerald Ellis was 67 when he made way in 1946 for a successor who would play a crucial role in shaping the future of the school, Geoffrey Marlar. Very much the man in charge, Marlar was one who enjoyed getting out and about, making a point of knowing all the boys in his charge. Soon to be of special interest to Raman was that Geoffrey Marlar had a cricketing son. One year older than Raman, Robin Marlar began to make his mark in cricket at Harrow at the same time as Raman was becoming the star of Whitgift. The two would later play together for Cambridge and become opposing county captains.

Robin Marlar remembers well the bedroom he had when at home with his parents, 'behind the bowler's arm looking out over the cricket field'. He recalls, too, that his father had much to do to get the school back on its feet, but there were compensations. 'The school was in a total mess, but it had two absolutely outstanding boys. One was an Indian boy called Subba Row and the other was a boy called Ian Beer.' Beer, like Raman, would go on to earn a CBE, playing rugby for England and becoming an outstanding headmaster, first at Ellesmere, then at Lancing and finally, from 1981 to 1991, at Harrow. The two are still members of what Dr Barnett regards as the most outstanding of all old boy year groups, keeping in the closest touch with their alma mater.

But what, beyond his cricketing prowess, made Raman of such special interest to Geoffrey Marlar? 'My father was always interested in the parents,' son Robin explains, citing the importance of Panguluri's position in legal circles at a time when cases were still pouring in to the Privy Council from India. 'With Gandhi in his pomp, the litigious Indians were going to law at the drop of a hat,' Robin continues. 'Raman's father really had an aura, a quite remarkable aura.'

With the end of the War bringing an influx of younger blood to the teaching staff, Raman regards himself as exceptionally lucky to have been at Whitgift at this time. It was a school in which he quickly made friends and, among the many congenial members of the teaching staff, he singles out Mr J.E.A. Blatherwick, a Yorkshireman known to the boys as 'Cod'. Though without first-class playing credentials, 'Cod' Blatherwick had opened the batting with some success for Cheltenham College in 1933 and later played for the Yorkshire Gentlemen and the Forty Club. But it was his infectious enthusiasm for the game of cricket that Raman recalls with gratitude. 'He encouraged me, he got me going.'

That enthusiasm received a boost in 1946 with the restoration of county cricket, and for Raman and his family there was the special attraction of a tour by India. In September the chance to see the tourists in action came at Hastings, where a closely fought match at the festival saw the Indians declare their second innings and go on to defeat the South by ten runs. The 14-year-old Raman remembers his father knocking nervously on the dressing room door at the close of play, keen to meet his compatriots. For Raman there was the thrill of shaking hands with Vijay Merchant, captain for the match, and other members of the team.

By the following summer Whitgift were to discover what a talented young cricketer they had acquired. By the age of 15 Raman had won a place in the first eleven, going on to be appointed captain in the last of his four years in the side. By his second year he was the leading batsman with an average of 27, a figure that rose next year to 43 and then to 48 in his final summer. There were two undefeated centuries in 1949 with his highest score of 120 coming in 1950. Meanwhile his bowling also went from strength to strength. Off breaks brought him ten wickets in 1948 and 37 in 1949, but the next year, when he switched to bowling leg breaks and googlies, his 52 wickets came at ten apiece and included a pair of nine-wicket hauls. Against Incogniti they cost 27, against Hurstpierpoint he conceded just nine runs.

Raman acknowledges a debt to George Fuller, his first professional at Whitgift, but he is effusive about Fuller's successor, the Surrey all-rounder Eddie Watts. 'He was terrific, he really was.' Watts knew the game intimately and Raman found his advice on batting technique very precise and thorough, and he was a constant source of titbits on wider aspects of the game. Given Raman's all-round record, it seems surprising that no place was found for him in the schools' representative games at Lord's, but his talents were known to his county. In 1949 he played five matches for Surrey Young Amateurs, making 106 at the Oval against Essex. The following year, fresh from school, he was included in the county's second eleven for the first time, scoring 21 not out against Gloucestershire.

Raman with Peter Price, Whitgift captain in 1948 and 1949

Though cricket grew to play a greater part in Raman's holidays, his childhood summers included long stretches at Normans Bay, eight miles from Eastbourne, where Doris and her sister, Raman's Aunt Katie, owned a bungalow. Set above a pebble and shingle beach with expansive sands at low tide, it was a blissful retreat, though close enough to the sea for occasional alarms when the tide was at its highest. Waves sometimes lapped the top of the steps that led down to the beach, but the bungalow itself was never flooded. Away from the beach, where Raman and his cousin Ann spent long hours, a vivid memory for Raman is as a 14-year-old standing in for the stationmaster at Normans Bay Halt. 'I'm off for a drink,' the stationmaster would say as he departed to the Star Inn, leaving Raman in charge of manning the level crossing gates. 'I knew all the train times,' he says, 'the slow ones stopped and the quick ones flashed through to Cooden Beach. Never in a million years should I have done it, but I grew up doing it regularly.'

2

'I hope you'll be very happy here'

A place at Trinity Hall

The thought that Raman might go up to Cambridge came not from Whitgift but a friend of the family, Russell Bailey, who lived near their Fairfield Road home and who suggested that he apply to Trinity Hall, Bailey's old college. It comes as a surprise to many that Trinity Hall is in no sense an annexe to the larger Trinity College located next door. In fact, Trinity Hall is the older of the two colleges, dating back to 1350 with only Peterhouse, Clare, Pembroke and Gonville & Caius claiming earlier foundations. Always a college with a strong law tradition, the inspiration for its founding by William Bateman, Bishop of Norwich, was his concern that the Black Death, especially severe in Norfolk and Suffolk, had deprived his diocese of clergy and lawyers. Hence at its foundation the College was designed solely for students of canon and civil law. Law was still where the College's academic heart lay when Raman applied. One of the smaller colleges that has since expanded with further off-site accommodation, principally for post-graduates, Trinity Hall has always been proud of its family atmosphere in which academics, students and staff coalesce into a body proud of the College and its traditions; and few can have maintained stronger links with alumni of all generations. Enviably sited on the river, along which undergraduates and visitors alike steer their punts, the Hall, as its members would refer to it, has a long cherished rowing tradition.

For an applicant with cricketing credentials Cambridge may have offered more relevant colleges, but among those in residence at Trinity Hall in 1950 was David Sheppard, a future Bishop of Liverpool, destined to captain the England team in 1954 and with whom, though he could not have guessed it at the time, Raman would play for two seasons for the University. Raman soon discovered that rowing was not the only sport to have its adherents at the Hall, when he attended for his initial interview.

This was with a man whom Raman grew to like enormously, the Reverend Owen Chadwick, at the time Dean of the College, but later to become Master of Selwyn College. By the time of his death in 2015 at the age of 99, his reputation had long been secure as one of the leading ecclesiastical scholars of his time, and he had the unusual distinction of holding successively the chairs of both Ecclesiastical and Modern History. A man of unfailing good humour and urbanity, Chadwick had won a Blue for rugby. If not a cricketer, he was an enthusiast for sport and one able to offer some balance against the all-pervading Boat Club culture. Raman remembers little detail of the interview, but he clearly made a favourable impression, Chadwick's parting words making clear that there would be a place for him. 'I hope you'll be very happy here,' he said.

So, in the autumn of 1950, Raman went up to Cambridge to read Law. The college he found was very much in the mould of its Master, Professor H.R. Dean. The last Oxbridge professor to exercise his right, in lieu of pension, to retain his professorial position until death, he had been elected Master of Trinity Hall as far back as 1929 and did not retire until 1954. Dean it was who nurtured the College's family ethos while enriching it with a range of gifted fellows who in turn inspired the undergraduates attending their supervisions. Generations of Hall men would recall the dedication of 'Daddy' Dean, as he was affectionately known, to all manner of College activities, not least in urging the Hall boats to further success as he bicycled along the tow path. Though his own specialism was pathology, Dean helped recruit and retain the fellows who maintained the College's supremacy in Law. Among those who supervised Raman was Tom Ellis Lewis, a leading expert in the law of Tort. Universally known as Tel, he was a remarkable Welshman who had used the proceeds of an industrial injury award to train himself to become a lawyer. Roman and Criminal Law were the preserve of J.W. Cecil Turner. A fellow of the College since 1926, Turner had been a cricketer, playing 46 matches for Worcestershire between 1911 and 1921, and he was for many years treasurer of the Cambridge University Cricket Club. An avowed atheist, it was with some difficulty that he had to reconcile himself to his daughter's choice of husband when she announced her engagement to Robert Runcie, later to become Archbishop of Canterbury, who succeeded Owen Chadwick as Dean of the College in 1956. It will have been some consolation that Runcie was himself an ardent follower of cricket, once invited to give the address at the annual *Wisden* lunch. Robert Runcie and his wife Lindy were later to become good friends of Raman and Anne, watching cricket together at Lord's and Canterbury, and with Anne sharing a love of the rose gardens that Lindy cultivated and tended at Lambeth Palace.

Raman soon settled into life at Trinity Hall. He was embarking on three of the most enjoyable years of his life and forging friendships that would endure into old age. Among those already in residence was Geoffrey Howe, later to become Chancellor of the Exchequer in the Thatcher government, with whose widow Elspeth the Subba Rows remain in touch, Raman having worked on the Broadcasting Standards Commission of which Lady Howe was at one time chairman. A friend in Raman's own year at Trinity Hall who shared his Indian roots was the Maharajah of Jaipur, known to all as Joey, whose hospitality Raman and Anne were to enjoy on their many trips to India in later life. Another contemporary in the 1950 intake was Bob Ely, now the College's representative assigned to keep in touch with all who arrived at the Hall that year, acting as the conduit through whom reports of achievements and activities are gathered and disseminated. A close friend of Raman and Anne Subba Row, he was indebted to Raman for finding the RAF Club as a venue for 30 or 40 of their contemporaries to meet up for a lunch each November, occasions that grew over the years by extending invitations to the Master of Trinity Hall and former dons of the College. Both Bob and Raman have further maintained their links with Trinity Hall through membership of the Aula Club, whose biannual dinners bring together old Hall men and women of all generations.

Bob Ely shares Raman's love of cricket, but offers as his only on-field distinction that he once captained a 14-year-old Ted Dexter at Radley. As in other colleges, it was customary for undergraduates to share rooms at Trinity Hall and Bob was happy to find himself paired up with a fellow modern linguist who happened also to be a talented cricketer, David Dickinson. Dickinson, had been in the first eleven for three years at Clifton College and was to win a Blue in his third year as an opening bowler, but it is as a bridge player that Bob remembers him well. The rooms they shared soon became the venue for a weekly game that would go on into the early hours, and Raman and Joey Jaipur were two of the regular four whom Dickinson assembled. Bob merely looked on. 'My main duty was to make coffee for them,' he says with a chuckle.

Not playing the game himself at Cambridge, Bob Ely paid five pounds to become a life member of the University Cricket Club, which brought him the privilege of sitting on top of the pavilion at Fenner's. There he would spend many hours, meeting a wide range of interesting people among them Cecil Turner, from whom he learnt how, as treasurer, he had negotiated for Oxford and Cambridge, with the fine cricketers the two universities were nurturing, to receive enhanced grants from MCC. Bob would often be joined by Raman and his team mates as they waited to bat.

Though Raman spent his first two terms yearning for the cricket season to come round, he was able to play some college rugby, where he was a fly half, but his principal winter sport was Rugby fives, a game he had learnt and enjoyed at Whitgift and at which he won a Blue in his first year. The Rugby version of fives entails playing in an enclosed court without the buttresses that characterise Eton and Winchester fives. In contrast to squash, a game Raman claims never to have mastered, it is played with a hard leather-covered ball and gloved hands. In each of his three years at Cambridge, the Light Blues emerged victorious against Oxford, in the last under Raman's captaincy with fellow cricketer Dennis Silk as secretary and destined to take over the following year.

The winter was also the time when those with aspirations to play cricket needed to ensure they did not fall behind in preparing for their examinations. 'It was not easy,' Raman now says, 'not being academic. I had to work, no question about that. I would never have got through without having worked.' When he left Cambridge, Raman had done well enough to be awarded a third class degree. A bachelor of arts on graduating, he later paid the small fee demanded by the University to upgrade to the status of MA.

The Latham Lawn at Trinity Hall from the terrace by the river

3

'In a tight spot I liked to see him go in'

Playing for Cambridge

The Cambridge cricket team in 1950 had been an exceptionally strong one with as distinguished a top four as can have been seen at Fenner's. John Dewes and David Sheppard had both enjoyed outstanding seasons, the highlight an opening stand of 343 against the West Indians. With their captain Hubert Doggart, they had been chosen for England that summer. At number four, the only one of the quartet to average below fifty, was Peter May, widely acknowledged as the finest player of them all whose Test debut would come in 1951. Dewes and Sheppard had toured Australia with MCC that winter. With them in Freddie Brown's party was John Warr, a pace bowler who played in two of the Tests. Warr now returned to Cambridge as captain with Sheppard, his designated successor, and May, both thirsting for more runs on Cyril Coote's fine batting pitches.

Of the other old Blues Mike Stevenson, soon to be a regular cricket writer for *The Daily Telegraph*, would be seeking to retain his place as a batsman, but as Raman awaited the chance to show his capabilities, he will have known that there were other batting spots waiting to be taken. In the traditional two-day trial match for freshmen Raman was chosen for Warr's XI against Sheppard's XI. An innings of 22 at number four in a total of 127 gave evidence of his ability before he fell to the wiles of another freshman who would make his mark that summer, Robin Marlar, son of his headmaster at Whitgift and an off spinner later mentioned in selection minutes at Lord's though destined never to win a Test cap. Marlar's three wickets that day were to be outshone by Raman when Sheppard's XI collapsed to his leg breaks. His four for 35 in a total of 111 for nine was followed by a second-innings 56, the only half-century of the match, then three more wickets as Warr's XI claimed victory by 15 runs. Raman's bridge friend David Dickinson also distinguished himself with first-innings figures that underlined the funereal pace of the match: 13 – 11 – 4 – 2.

Dickinson would have to wait two years to make his first-class debut, only Raman and Marlar among the 22 freshmen winning a place in the side for the opening match against Lancashire. There followed a disheartening time for the Cambridge team and for Raman. His first-class baptism emphasised the gulf the 19-year-old faced between school and first-class cricket as he scored only a single before being caught and bowled by Bob Berry; but for the whole team there was the frustration of rain that rendered the first three matches draws in which neither side batted twice. A top score for his side of 33 against Essex was the only consolation in a period when there was little call on Raman's bowling. Omitted from the side that lost heavily to Yorkshire, he was tried unsuccessfully as an opener against Sussex. There was a thrilling draw with Middlesex, when the match ended with the county needing just one more run with their last pair together, but two Cambridge declarations had denied Raman a chance to bat. By the final home match, against Free Foresters, he was batting at number eight. He departed Fenner's with just 52 first-class runs and he had taken only two wickets in six matches.

In an era when Oxford and Cambridge played a full programme of first-class matches it was a challenge to the university sides that their senior players, in particular, would be called away to face the bowling of the examiners in the first half of the season, whilst the earlier matches also saw the counties sharpening their teeth for the Championship and disinclined to rest their top players. As Cambridge set off on tour the side was without a win, but there had been only a single loss against seven drawn games. Better times lay ahead.

Already May and, when his academic studies allowed him to play, Sheppard had been in imperious form. This year they averaged for Cambridge 71.44 and 49.55 respectively at a time when first-class runs were not as freely earned as in more modern times. With a stronger side assembled for the tour, there were now three wins in four matches. At Worcester Raman was 'flighting his leg breaks in skilful fashion' to take four for 37 in the first innings, helping

Fenner's

pave the way to a four-wicket win. However, he had again failed with the bat – he was now averaging just 7.86 – but this was soon to change.

Against Sussex at Worthing Cambridge won the toss and chose to bat, but were soon in trouble. With Sheppard out early for 2, fellow opener Pat Mathews succumbing for a duck and May dismissed for 4, there had been a partial recovery when Raman joined John Cockett at 94 for four. Cockett was a friend from Trinity Hall now in his final year, destined to make his name as a Great Britain hockey player, for whom this innings brought his only first-class century. A sparkling stroke-maker, he made merry as Raman contributed 32 to their partnership of 115.

John Cockett remembers their alliance that day, commenting that he and Raman were soulmates in that team. Though senior in years, Cockett still felt something of a newcomer in a team dominated by the infectious enthusiasm of John Warr and with a number of established players from earlier years. 'Raman was such a delightful person. With John Warr the life and soul of the party, some of us as newcomers didn't feel quite so much at ease. Raman never pushed himself forward. He and I and one or two others were more retiring. We were new boys and we knew our place!'

Raman was in the runs again in the second innings, an undefeated 44 helping set up a second declaration, after which Sussex collapsed meekly for 79 to the pace bowling of Olly Wait (six for 18) to give Cambridge victory by 137 runs. Sheppard and May then paraded their batting skills against a weakened Surrey attack at Guildford in a drawn match before Cambridge tasted further success, trouncing MCC at Lord's by 322 runs, with a now more confident Raman making 77 not out in the second innings before Warr and Wait demolished the home club for 43. The victory march was interrupted at Bournemouth where, after holding Hampshire on first innings, thanks to an undefeated 178 from May, the Light Blues folded in their second innings to concede defeat by 89 runs.

The match with Oxford now loomed with Raman having overcome his slow start to command a place in the side. There was just one further game ahead of the Varsity Match, a two-day fixture against The Army at RMA Sandhurst. With several talented national servicemen such as Micky Stewart and Brian Close in the Army side, this was no easy game, but it provided a platform for Raman to post an undefeated 100 as Cambridge had the better of a drawn game that sadly could not qualify for first-class status.

Cambridge came to Lord's in confident mood. They were the stronger side on paper and could point to a superior record, Oxford's only win having come at the expense of a Free Foresters side of modest pretentions. Winning the toss, Oxford chose to bat. Though their captain, South African Murray Hofmeyr, made 40 and Donald Carr 34, the rest succumbed to the bowling of Warr and Marlar as the innings closed on 178. The expected lead did not materialise. Both Sheppard and May fell when apparently well set and it was Raman who top-scored with 37 not out. It took him the best part of two hours, but with two foolish tail-end run outs Cambridge closed ten runs adrift. A gritty 80 in four hours and fifty minutes from England rugby international Brian Boobbyer and a less cautious 50 from Carr meant that Cambridge, let down by some shoddy fielding, would need 219 to win. That it was not more was largely due to Raman, whose leg breaks brought him five for 21, the best figures of his first-class career.

Again Cambridge's star batsmen threatened to make light work of the target. Sheppard, with 42, and May, 33, looked in command, but at 127 for five both were gone. Raman soon followed and only some resolute hitting by Australian Bill Hayward and Marlar brought the target within sight, Oxford winning by 21 runs with 17 minutes to spare as the future India Test player Ramesh Divecha ended with seven for 62. *Playfair*, still finding space for a full report of the match, suggested that Cockett, had he come off, might have turned the match. Sadly his contribution was a pair, as it was to be on his next appearance at Lord's. As he delights in reminding his friends, the scorer was again little troubled when he was chosen for a Minor Counties XI against the Australians in 1953. 'I still have nightmares about it,' he admits over 60 years later.

Sixth in the batting averages with 22.61 and with 15 wickets at 24.66, Raman had justified the faith Warr must have had in him. At the end of the Varsity match the team elected their officers for the following summer. Invariably a freshman would be chosen as secretary and would expect to be captain in his final year. There were two candidates: Raman and Marlar, who now recalls how he came to be chosen. 'I had probably had marginally the better match, but I suspect Raman slipping away on Sundays may have told against him. I don't know.' A feature of Raman's summer had been his determination to continue playing whenever he could for the Stoics, a wandering side for whom he had played a few games as a schoolboy. In Marlar's view it was evidence of Raman's loyalty, a laudable Indian trait; but it had happened in the face of strong opposition from his Cambridge captain. 'John Warr told him "I don't want you doing it." But he took no notice. Every Sunday he went, having been told expressly not to do so.'

Marlar believes that Raman's leg breaks were of particular value to the wandering side. 'He used to get five wickets probably every Sunday. He didn't really spin it, but he was very accurate.' Apart from club cricket, Raman now had a couple of matches for Surrey Second XI. In the win against Hampshire he played little part, but top-scored against Essex at Chingford with 65 as he got an early taste of playing alongside many who would soon be colleagues for Surrey and, in the case of Ken Barrington and Roy Swetman, England.

For Raman's second year, Sheppard, now captain, and May were again the leading lights, while former captain Warr returned for a fourth year. Though his bowling was not quite as successful as hitherto, he now had an opening partner with recent Test experience in the South African Cuan McCarthy. As wicket-keeper there was Gerry Alexander, later to captain West Indies, while Gerry Tordoff, another freshman, had shown his capabilities as a batsman in a few matches for Somerset. In a summer where both May and Sheppard averaged over 70, Raman, with 41.31, was comfortably the next in the list. His figures reflected a remarkably consistent season in which he was not once dismissed for a single figure score. Yet the ability to convert useful starts into match-winning innings seemed to elude him: until the Varsity Match he had passed 50 just four times. Nevertheless, in his captain's eyes, Raman 'was beginning to show the calmness and concentration which later made him an England player.'

For the Light Blues it was another season of frustration. At Fenner's they were several times on the brink of victory: Leicestershire hung on for a draw with one wicket left; against Essex only 12 were needed with three wickets in hand; Yorkshire were grateful to have three wickets still standing when the match ended with their batsmen requiring another 70; in the Middlesex match an improbable last wicket stand left Cambridge seeking 90 in 55 minutes and falling six runs short with four wickets to fall. When victory came at last, against Free Foresters in the final home match, it was by an innings and 86 runs.

On tour the Sussex match was lost after Cambridge, in a dominant position, became the victims of Sheppard's generous declaration. Against Surrey at the Oval May was absent on Test match duty and Sheppard was also unable to play as the county champions, even with a weakened attack, won by an innings and 40 runs. May was still absent as Warwickshire, having been forced to follow on, turned the tables so comprehensively that it was Cambridge hanging on with eight wickets down after a Sheppard century had suggested that a challenging target of 231 at 92 an hour might be achieved. It was Sheppard again at Worcester, where the elusive first defeat of a county came with the Cambridge captain undefeated on 239 in pursuit of 375 at 75 an hour. A vital partnership was with Raman, whose 68 helped add 202. Throughout his career solidity was seen as Raman's principal virtue, but he was now starting to reveal a wider range of shots.

Against Gloucestershire, where Raman top-scored with 88, a personal best, it was the last pair holding the fort for Cambridge to avert defeat.

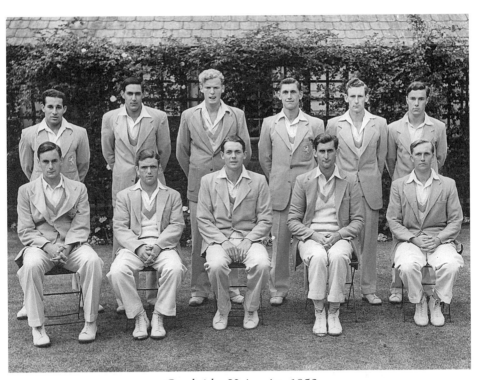

Cambridge University, 1952

FCM Alexander, R Subba Row, CN McCarhy, GG Tordoff, CJM Kenny, MH Bushby
PBH May, RG Marlar, DS Sheppard, JJ Warr, MH Stevenson

A two-day match with MCC was spoilt by rain, after which Cambridge awaited an Oxford side that had endured a dismal season in which only a youthful Colin Cowdrey had suggested the talent for a career beyond university. But cricket is a game that readily makes fools of those who indulge in predictions. Oxford, batting first on a benign pitch, exuded caution, and it was not until the second day that they were dismissed for 272, Marlar ending with seven for 104. That Cambridge overhauled this score was almost entirely thanks to 127 from their captain and 94 from Raman. Sheppard would later write of his partner: 'I always enjoyed batting with Raman. He had great composure and determination and greatly added to his power of stroke (this year) though he was never an exciting player to watch. But if we were in a tight spot I liked to see him go in. We had just that situation against Oxford and he did not let us down.' Raman had been on 62 at the start of the third day. With the call for quick runs, *Playfair* commented that he had 'forced the pace in handsome style' and 'sacrificed his wicket in the cause.'

For Oxford, 136 behind, it was a matter of batting the day out and hoping to build a lead that could not be overhauled. At 127 for seven with 90 minutes to go their cause looked lost, but opening bowler Alan Coxon, a left-hander with both bat and ball, now mounted a rearguard action that has gone down in the legends of Varsity Match cricket. Throwing his bat at the ball, he ensured that runs would play a part in the equation not simply time. McCarthy had unsettled the early batsmen with pace and lift, but all he and Warr threw at Coxon was repelled or taken on the body without flinching as, helped by Australian Alan Dowding, he built a lead of 43, at which point, with quarter of an hour to play, Sheppard admitted the game had been put well beyond his side's reach.

Raman had played a full part in a season that had seen him mature as a batsman, though his bowling was increasingly becoming a second string. 'To be honest I wasn't a very good bowler anyway,' he now says, 'and I soon realised that it was a better game if you were a batsman!' There had been five for 87 against Yorkshire and three for 23 against the Indians, but as the season wore on Sheppard made less and less use of Raman and his haul was only 18 wickets at 35.94. So it was something of a surprise to find that his two games for Surrey Second XI should yield figures of 30.2 – 9 – 60 – 11. Might this not be one for 60, I wondered? But *Wisden* is indeed to be trusted. Against Cornwall at Beddington Park, Wallington, Raman's figures were an astonishing 7.2 – 5 – 4 – 7.

For Raman's final year at Cambridge he and Robin Marlar were, in the words of *Wisden*, 'the only two players of anything approaching top ranking claims.' Marlar would be captain, Raman his deputy. Sheppard, May and Warr had moved on into the county game, while McCarthy and Tordoff had also departed after just one year at the University. Of other old Blues Alexander remained as wicket-keeper, while Hayward responded well to the challenge of leading the attack and Mike Bushby, now the secretary, emerged from the shadow of David Sheppard to make a more solid contribution as an opening batsman. He was soon being partnered by Dennis Silk, another with an impressive school record who had been given few opportunities in 1952.

Above all Cambridge looked to Raman for runs. With 937 at 52.05 he did not fail them, and he went into the Varsity Match standing fourth in the national averages. An auspicious 64 came in the second match at Fenner's against Surrey's full-strength attack. If his future colleagues saw the best of Raman that day, he made sure that they saw the best of Cambridge after close of play. It certainly made a mark with the Bedser twins whose book *Following On*, published the following year, recalled their experience: 'An interesting evening was spent touring the colleges, our guides being Robin Marlar and

Raman in the nets

Raman Subba Row. The gardens and squares were a sight to behold, and there can be few cities so fair in the spring of the year. We thought how fortunate the undergraduates were to play their early cricket in such perfect conditions and surroundings.'

Another early match provided Robin Marlar with his outstanding memory of a season in which he had relished captaining the side: 'Bowling the Australians out before tea on the first day.' *Wisden* suggests it was a little later in the day, and the records say the whole innings took 108 overs, still a tribute to the speed at which the undergraduates bowled their overs with Marlar and Raman to the fore. At whatever hour tea may have been taken, there was time for Cambridge to reach 48 for 2 that evening, but for Marlar the abiding memory is of Keith Miller, 'whom I absolutely adored.' Miller had opened the batting, made a breezy 20 then departed for Newmarket races. Without mobile phones to alert him to the fall of wickets, he was startled to find his side all out for 383 on his return. Then, in Marlar's words: 'He threw his clothes on, flies all undone, shirt undone, hair undone, came straight down to where there were two distinguished masters of colleges having tea at Joan

Coote's bar at the end of the pavilion. With one hand Miller swept all the tea off their plates, grabbed the sugar bowl and put the contents in his pocket. "Sorry, I've lost my shirt and I'm absolutely starving!"' The two masters, Marlar later discovered, had been happily discussing an experiment they had conducted behind the lines in the First World War to discover how far a crystal set would transmit.

The match against the Australians was lost by an innings, Raman top-scoring in the second innings. There were five half-centuries at Fenner's before the elusive maiden hundred came against MCC. If this was an undemanding innings, setting up a declaration against a modest attack in a match that was ultimately lost, there were no such reservations with his 146 not out against Nottinghamshire at Trent Bridge a fortnight later. The runs came in a second innings rearguard action with Australian Bruce Dooland, the country's leading leg spinner, operating in tandem with Gamini Goonesena, a bowler of similar mode. A stand of 220 with Alexander, who fell one short of his century, almost enabled Cambridge to save a match in which they had trailed by 184 on first innings.

That summer saw three wins for the Light Blues against seven losses ahead of the Varsity Match. There had been a three-wicket success against Middlesex at Fenner's when Vincent Lumsden, a freshman from Jamaica, led the charge to take full advantage of a sporting declaration, victory coming with three minutes to spare. Free Foresters were beaten by 190 runs, and a third win came on tour when Kent were defeated by 134 runs at Folkestone, Marlar returning match figures of 13 for 90 and Raman top-scoring in each innings with 57 and 71.

Oxford came to Lord's without a single win, but it was the Dark Blues in command in the first half of the match. Cowdrey's 116, with strokes all round the wicket, was the dominant contribution as poor Cambridge catching allowed Oxford to reach 312, to which Cambridge replied with only 191, no batsman making more than 31. Marlar had taken five for 94 in the first innings and his off spinners now brought Cambridge back into the match. With seven for 49 he was the principal destroyer as Oxford collapsed to 116 all out, Cowdrey now falling for a duck. Cambridge had over five hours in which to make 238. Silk dropped anchor as he saw his partners come and go, the most productive of them Raman with 28 in his final innings for the University. With 35 minutes left Marlar joined Silk at 182 for eight in what seemed to be a bid to save the game. Then Silk took 19 in one over from left-arm spinner Jimmy Allan. He ended on 116 as he steered his side home from the fifth ball of what would have been the penultimate over. It was Cambridge's first win over Oxford since 1949.

4

'£600 expenses or you can't come'

Commonwealth tour of India

Immediately after the Varsity Match Raman hastened to Birmingham, where he was to make his first team debut for Surrey. The county that had won the Championship the previous year by a margin of 32 points was finding life less easy in 1953. The middle order batting was feeling the loss of Laurie Fishlock and Jack Parker, who had both retired, and Raman made an ideal replacement for the former, also a left-hander. Though the Warwickshire match was lost, Raman was soon playing a full part in Surrey's eventual retention of the title by 16 points. There were half-centuries in comprehensive victories over Worcestershire and Leicestershire. A loss to Gloucestershire at Bristol was followed by a rain-spoiled match against the Australians, after which came perhaps the most crucial win of the season when Nottinghamshire were defeated at the Oval by six runs. Two Surrey declarations deprived Raman of an innings, but he could still claim to have played the crucial role at the death. As the final over began, Nottinghamshire needed seven runs to win with their last pair at the wicket. To add to the excitement, John Kelly was carrying an injury and had a runner. From the first ball the runner saw the chance of a sharp single, but Raman flung the ball to wicket-keeper Arthur McIntyre, who broke the wicket just before his partner could make his ground.

Raman hit a much needed 83 in a win against Hampshire. Then, after a drawn game against Middlesex at Lord's, he was the toast of his side at Loughborough, scoring his first century for his county. His 128 took five hours and included 19 fours, but despite his efforts Leicestershire managed to salvage a draw. While Surrey's principal bowlers were recovering the Ashes for England at the Oval, a second string attack was being put to the sword at Headingley. Rain had the final say with Surrey's first innings still uncompleted, but not before Raman's 56 had been top score for his side. Then it was on to Northampton, where Raman played an innings that may have helped shape his future in the game. Against an attack that included the pace of a raw Frank Tyson and the wiles of the Australian left-arm spinner George Tribe he posted his second century for Surrey, a faultless innings of 125. The runs had been badly needed, Raman coming to the wicket after both openers had been dismissed for ducks. There was a brisk undefeated 54 as Surrey declared a second time, but with time lost to rain their bowlers were unable to force a victory.

Four draws in succession was hardly the form of champions, though with two games in hand Surrey were still well placed, four points behind the leaders Leicestershire. Middlesex, in second place two points ahead of Surrey, had also played two more matches when the sides met at the Oval. Raman was unable to play in this crucial match, which took Surrey back to the top of the table, but he played a part in the triumphant finale to the season. Scores of 59 and 47 not out helped in the 171-run defeat of Glamorgan. Then, following a draw with Sussex, the outcome of other matches ensured that the title was already sealed before Hampshire were defeated by nine wickets at Bournemouth.

Often in the stand at the Oval watching Raman as he made his first contributions to the successful Surrey side was his mother. Doris's regular companion was Mary Webb, mother of John, a teenager who went on to captain Whitgift in 1956. John Webb recalls how the pressure could be too much for Doris: 'When Raman was batting, she was so nervous that she used to go to the ladies' loo. She could still hear the crowd's reactions and applause and my mother, posted outside the ladies' loo, had to tell her what had happened and whether Raman had survived a narrow escape or hit a boundary.'

Raman ended the season with an average of 53.86 in championship matches, second only to May's 57.23. In the overall first-class list only James Langridge, with just ten innings, Len Hutton, Australian Jock Livingston of Northants and May were ahead of him. Raman's stellar performances sparked interest from an unexpected quarter when he received a telephone call from George Duckworth, former Lancashire and England wicket-keeper, who had subsequently embarked on a career in journalism. 'He said, "I'm taking a Commonwealth team to India this winter. Would you like to come?" He told me he could only afford to give me £600. I was staggered. I said, "I'm an amateur. I can't take that sort of money." He said, "You'll have to take £600 expenses or you can't come."'

For Raman it was a chance to defer thinking about what he might do to earn a living that winter and it was an opportunity to visit for the first time the country of his father's birth and upbringing. Concerns about amateur status conveniently shelved, Raman accepted Duckworth's offer. The first Commonwealth tour had come about in 1949/50 when MCC had withdrawn from plans for making a similar visit to India, and such was the popularity of the substitute tour with the Indian public that it was repeated the following winter. There followed an official MCC tour under Nigel Howard in 1951/52. Now Duckworth was undertaking his third visit. Styled the Silver Jubilee Tour, it was to mark the 25th anniversary of the Indian Board of Control, and of its 21 matches five would again be unofficial Tests against a full-strength India team. These ventures owed much to Duckworth's meticulous planning and management. Both his earlier tours, the first captained by Jock Livingston and the second by Les Ames, had been successes on the field as well as off, but this would be a fourth tour of the Indian subcontinent in five seasons and it was to be undertaken with a rather weaker team.

The captain was Ben Barnett. Now aged 45, he had toured England as a wicket-keeper with the 1938 Australians. His leading players were Frank Worrell and Sonny Ramadhin, both of whom had to leave before the third unofficial Test to play for their own West Indies team against England in the Caribbean. Worrell's batting was certainly missed, though Ramadhin, a success on the previous tour, had failed to take a wicket in either of the first two Tests. Of the other batsmen in the party Reg Simpson was in imperious form, but he too had to depart the tour early, leaving only the Australian Ken Meuleman and, to a lesser degree, Roy Marshall, soon to join Hampshire, as serious run-makers.

The pace attack comprised a young Peter Loader and the Australian Sam Loxton with Lancashire's Bob Berry the principal spinner. Jack Iverson, Australia's mystery spinner, was one of those who flew in as a replacement and played a major part in the Commonwealth side's only Test victory. But the rump of the party comprised worthies from the English county game, most of whom struggled to rise to the challenge of international cricket. No fewer than 20 different players took some part in the tour, and among replacements flown out was another Barnett, 43-year-old Charlie of Gloucestershire, who had retired five years earlier. Only three matches were won against five losses with 13 drawn games, a comment on the nature of many of the pitches. India took the unofficial Test series by two matches to one.

Where earlier teams had enjoyed three weeks at sea, Duckworth had now opted to fly. When Raman joined the party that boarded a Comet jet liner at Heathrow, it was his first taste of air travel and he was taking his seat on a plane that was at the forefront in providing new levels of passenger comfort. Arriving in India in early October, Raman played in 14 matches, ending fifth in the averages with 42.66. He started the tour with 77 not out against the Cricket Club of India at the gracious Brabourne Stadium in what was then Bombay. There was a second 77 against Combined Universities at Bangalore and Raman made the same score for a third time when undefeated in his final knock, against the Prime Minister's XI at Calcutta. His only other score above fifty came at Amritsar, where he made 72 against North Zone.

Though Raman's overall statistics may appear satisfactory, he was suffering a lean period at the time when the various departures meant that places in the Test side might have been opening up. At 21 he was by some way the youngest member of the party and this may have contributed to a reluctance

Bound for India

BA Barnett, PA Gibb, GA Edrich (hidden), R Subba Row, R Berry,
GM Emmett, JE McConnon, G Duckworth, DW Barrick, JF Crapp,
PJ Loader, DGW Fletcher, FMM Worrell, KT Ramadhin, RE Marshall

to play him in any of the unofficial Tests. So it was that Geoff Edrich, George Emmett, David Fletcher and Charlie Barnett all gained precedence for a few matches despite achieving very little. Des Barrick, with whom Raman would soon be playing at Northants, won a place in the second Test, where his century was his only substantial score in the series, and if the selectors fancied a left-hander in the middle of the order, they had their man once Allan Watkins had been flown in and immediately struck form.

For Raman, who has developed a deep love of India, it was fascinating to see for the first time the country of which he had heard his father so often speak. 'I must have seen more of India than 99.9% of Indians. It was wonderful going down from Calcutta to where my father came from.' The team's earlier travels around India had mainly been by train, but this long journey to Madras after the third unofficial Test was by air. To reach the area where his father's family was based and to meet his aunt, Panguluri's sister, for the first time entailed a train journey up the coast to Guntur in the state of Andhra Pradesh, at the time a city of fewer than 200,000 but now boasting a population of more than three-quarters of a million. Meeting the extended family was a daunting encounter as Raman found himself without a common language with most of his relatives, many of whom he would meet again on future visits to India. Back home Raman was able to share his experiences with his parents, but sadly he was to lose a much loved father within weeks of his return, Panguluri's death on 20 March coming as great shock to the family. Raman's mother would live on in the Fairfield Road home until her death on 9 April 1972.

Raman was later to write of this first tour that 'one moment we were enjoying the grandeur of the Cricket Club of India or the Maharajah of Baroda's palace, the next we were fighting the rats and the cockroaches in some very inferior town hotel.' The match against the Cricket Club of India, where the tour began, was notable not just for the runs Raman made in a game where the tourists had much the better of a draw, but also for his first meeting with a friend with whom he has remained in touch ever since. Madhav Apte, India's Test opener in their recent series in the West Indies, had played for the home club, though with little success on this occasion, but it was through him that Raman was one day to become an Honorary Life Member of the CCI and enjoy the privilege of staying there when visiting India.

This same Madhav, in 2016, explained how his long-enduring friendship with Raman had first begun. As he spoke, his smiling eyes and easy movement belied his 84 years – they told more of an all-round sportsman whose passion for cricket saw him play his last game at the age of 80. It had all begun in childhood, and by his late teenage years cricket practice might be preceded by tennis at 6.30 in the morning, then a couple of games of badminton with his mother while the air remained still. At college there could be a table tennis match. 'Then after cricket practice in the afternoon, I would have a game of squash in the evening at the CCI.'

Proficient at all the sports mentioned and a champion at squash, Madhav made his mark in cricket at Elphinstone College, where his coach was already one of his idols, Vinoo Mankad. Madhav had been a leg break and googly bowler rather than a batsman, once taking ten for 10 in an important Giles Shield school match. 'I went in next to the roller,' he says, admitting some apprehension against fast bowing. It was Mankad who first suggested that he should try his hand as an opening bat. The runs flowed and he played for the Combined Universities against Nigel Howard's MCC team. Then an injury at practice to another of his childhood heroes and friends, the great Vijay Merchant, catapulted Madhav into the Bombay team for the Ranji Trophy. A century in his first match followed by other good scores led to speculation that he might win a place in the India team touring England the following summer.

Madhav was not chosen in the official party. 'But I went as a sort of camp follower,' he explains. 'Travel round with the team and play if you get the opportunity,' Merchant had advised him. So, with Madhav Mantri and Hemu Adhikari deputed to keep an eye on him, the 19-year-old's pilgrimage began when he, like Raman with the Commonwealth team, took his first flight in an aeroplane. There were five stops in the 24-hour journey to London. It was all a bit more adventurous, not to say hazardous, than it has become. 'The thirteenth row of seats was called 12A in those days,' he recalls. One of the tourists' early matches was at Fenner's. Madhav had a natural interest in the Anglo-Indian playing for Cambridge, though it was Peter May's 92 that made a deeper impression than Raman's 20. Madhav recalls that Raman's parents were also on the ground to watch their son, though to his great regret he never met Panguluri and Doris. Nor did he make Raman's acquaintance until the visit to India of the Commonwealth team.

By this time Madhav had benefited from the weak performance of India's batsmen on the tour of England, when they had capitulated to Fred Trueman's pace. A new opener was clearly needed and, after making his Test debut on his home ground against Pakistan, Madhav had been selected for the tour of West Indies. It wasn't just the cricket that made its mark. 'We enjoyed such wonderful hospitality out there. So I said that when people come here I wanted to do the same.' Madhav's kindness back in 1953 gave Raman his first visit to what the Aptes then called 'the bungalow'. Set in nearly three acres of gardens and woodlands, their home had stables for cattle and horses as well as a tennis court and an area for cricket practice. Now Madhav lives at the same address, but he and his wife Sheela, with three further generations

Martin Pullon, England supporter, with Madhav Apte, 2016

of the Apte family, occupy the top floors of a 25-storey condominium built on the site. It is a home to which Mother Teresa once took the lift when visiting the school across the road that bears her name.

Over the years Raman and Anne have maintained regular contact with the Apte family, though it was at one time Madhav's late brother Arvind of whom they saw more. Also an opening batsman, Arvind edged his brother out of the position of reserve to Pankaj Roy and Nari Contractor on India's 1959 tour of England, when he made his sole Test appearance at Leeds. It was Arvind in whose name an apartment in a block overlooking Lord's was first registered in the 1960s. They acquired the property at a time when Madhav was beginning to make more business trips to London, and he remembers registering his disappointment, in Raman's presence, to Sir Paul Getty that his view of play should have been impaired by the canopy peaks of the new Mound stand Sir Paul had helped to finance.

Raman's life membership of the Cricket Club of India came while Madhav was president of the club, a position in which he succeeded Vijay Merchant in 1986. To mark the club's Golden Jubilee, the committee invited 50 international sportsmen, mainly cricketers, to become honorary life members. The first of these was Sir Donald Bradman, whose letter of acceptance is retained on display in the club. Raman's credentials may have been less illustrious than those of Sir Donald, but he was an international cricketer of distinction with Indian blood and a great affinity for the country. Life membership was an honour well merited that he was delighted and proud to accept.

Evening at The Cricket Club of India, Mumbai

The CCI was intended by its founders to be 'the MCC of Indian cricket'. As such it has been described as 'a private club with a public purpose'. Just as MCC owns Lord's, so do the members of the CCI own the Brabourne Stadium, which was opened in 1937. Named after a former Governor of Bombay, who was an enthusiastic sponsor of the cause, the ground should have staged its first Test match against England in the season of 1939/40, but Hitler's intervention delayed it until December 1948 when the match against West Indies ended in a run feast of a draw.

Like MCC's Lord's with its real tennis and squash courts, the CCI offers members more than the best seats to watch the cricket. It, too, has squash courts and has staged lawn tennis competitions and hockey matches on the outfield, but the spacious pavilion has more of the atmosphere of a traditional gentlemen's club, with its everyday dining facilities and its billiard room with three full-size tables. Yet it is still cricket at the heart of the club with pictures of the great teams and players of the past lining the walls and rooms bearing the names of such folk heroes as Polly Umrigar. Though there may now be less cricket to watch, the aura of the Raj still pervades as members enjoy a sundowner in the comfort of the wicker chairs brought out in front of the pavilion each evening. Like a Pall Mall club, too, the CCI has bedroom accommodation not only for members but for visiting teams, the only Test match ground in the world able to offer such facilities.

Among those to have spoken rapturously about the club is Keith Miller, whose words paint a picture of a lost age: 'Players can live on it during the match. At night a complete dance floor is carried out and put down over the playing area. There under the soft Indian night with millions of stars twinkling overhead you can waltz to the strains of a carefully concealed orchestra. When you feel the need for refreshments you walk a few yards to a perfectly equipped bar. In the morning you get out of bed and look down on a pitch where a few hours later you will be playing.'

For Raman and Anne the prospect of visiting the CCI was always enriched by the certainty of being warmly welcomed and entertained by Raj Singh Dungarpur, a legendary figure around the club for many years, who succeeded Madhav Apte as its president in 1992. Manager of the India team to England in 1982, Raj Singh later became president of the Board of Control for Cricket in India and played an important part in getting foreign coaches to take charge of the national team. His death in 2009 prompted Sachin Tendulkar to propose that his name be remembered, as one of the great benefactors of Indian cricket, by naming the refurbished main gate in his honour, a project which came to fruition in 2016.

Raj Singh with Raman

That the Brabourne Stadium no longer stages Test cricket despite its 45,000 seat capacity is one of cricket's tragedies, and here again the history of its loss has echoes of Lord's, MCC and the TCCB/ECB, where a members' club and a governing body have differing priorities in laying on major matches. If the ECB were to raise funds to build their own new ground in, say, Regents Park, and turn their back on Lord's, it would be the modern equivalent of the Bombay Cricket Association's decision to desert the Brabourne for their own poorly designed and scruffy Wankhede built close by, where spectators are packed into an arena that offers them only very basic facilities. It could never happen, they all said at the time, but it did. And it happened despite the efforts of Madhav Apte to accommodate the Association's plea for a greater allocation of seats for the big matches at the Brabourne. It left the Brabourne home to as gracious a gentlemen's club as ever, cherished by Raman and Anne as their Mumbai bolthole, but a backwater for top-class cricket.

The Apte family are not the only members of the Indian cricketing fraternity to retain close links with the Subba Rows. Also opposing Raman on the Commonwealth tour and in the party touring England in 1952 was C.D. Gopinath. At 86 'Gopi' Gopinath is second only to Dattu Gaekwad as India's oldest living Test cricketer. Yet the bounce in his stride as he entered the hotel lobby for our rendezvous was unmistakeably that of the 22-year-old described in *Playfair* as a fast outfielder. Roll him a ball across the marble floor and he would surely still have been able to swoop upon it and startle the concierge with a bail-high throw.

Regular guests of Gopi and his wife Comi, Raman and Anne were early visitors to their cottage at Coonoor in the Nilgiri hills, where the Gopinaths escape the oppressive heat of Chennai's summer. It is thanks to Gopi that they have been able to visit the birthplace of Raman's father. The hospitality has been returned when Gopi and Comi have visited England, as they did for many years, the annual business trip carefully timed for the middle of June to take in the Lord's Test, where Gopi can make use of his MCC membership, and then Wimbledon, catering for Comi's special passion. Gopi too was brought up on tennis. When he boarded at Madras Christian College, the third generation of his family to attend the school, his other sports were football and hockey. Then, aged 17, he found the cricket team looking for a wicket-keeper. 'Why not you?' they suggested. So Gopi practised in the nets and became, for the first time, a cricketer. 'Then the opening batsman was failing all the time,' he remembers. 'So the captain said, "You go and open." I made sixty or so and some other scores. Four years later I was playing for India!'

Winning his first Test cap against Nigel Howard's tourists, Gopi took the last catch as India registered their first ever victory over England, winning by an innings and eight runs in the final match of the series. It was in his home city of Madras that this milestone in history was achieved, and Gopi speaks with some sadness as he reflects on the changes he has seen at his beloved Chepauk ground in what is now Chennai. In Gopi's playing days a tree-lined ground admitting the sea breeze to pass through temporarily erected stands, it has become a cauldron of a stadium second in size only to Eden Gardens, Kolkata. The felling of so many trees in the construction of the modern stadium especially pains Gopi, just as he had been saddened, only days before our meeting in December 2016, by his city's loss of ten thousand trees to Cyclone Varda, one of them blocking access from his home.

Gopi's rich experience of cricket includes witnessing, from the comfort of number seven in the batting order, India's infamous second innings slide to 0 for four at Headingley in 1952. There were few runs for him that summer and just the one Test, but in the county games he hared around the outfield. 'So many of the cricketers were from the privileged classes,' he recalls. 'They were used to batting and bowling, but they had servants to do the fielding.' Now obliged to field for themselves, the older members of the side stood and dropped catches in the slips, Gopi remembers, while he and other youngsters had to do the hard work in the deep.

As Gopi talks we enjoy dinner in the serenity of the Madras Club, familiar to Raman and Anne. Now housed in a gracious building from the late 18th century, it was at one time the exclusive refuge of the ex-pat British. 'They used to wear black tie for committee meetings,' Gopi explains, 'and you had to wear a suit and tie to eat.' Now standards of dress may have relaxed, but the club still caters for anglophiles who relish an essentially English menu bereft of oriental spices. There are tennis courts and a swimming pool, and it is a haven for those like Gopi and Raman who enjoy a game of bridge. 'Yes, Raman is a very good player,' Gopi confirms.

The conversation moves on to the future of the game. 'Don't call it cricket. Give it some other name,' Gopi pleads as we agree that the twenty-over game is now the money-spinner. Nothing has saddened him more than the match fixing and corruption that has found its way into cricket. 'With money all the evils have come into the game,' he asserts. Now he finds players of the past 30 years in an air-conditioned cocoon almost oblivious of how the game was once played. 'If we played in Delhi, we were billeted out for Tests,' he says, going on to recall less luxurious accommodation. 'I remember once we all spent the nights in a railway carriage parked in a siding – with all our bags!'

5

'Why don't you come and play for us?'

From Surrey to Northants

Back with Surrey, Raman joined a side on its way to the third of what would become seven consecutive championships. Surrey's start had not suggested that they would retain their title, but an astonishing run in which eight of their last nine matches were won enabled them to finish 22 points ahead of Yorkshire. The transformation in form owed most to the bowling of Jim Laker and Tony Lock, who seemed determined to show the MCC selectors the folly of choosing others to tour Australia, while the dynamic leadership of Stuart Surridge forced victory from some unpromising situations. For Raman there were three half-centuries in the first four matches followed by an unbeaten 117 against Somerset at the Oval in early June, but never thereafter did he pass fifty. Runs, especially at the Oval, were always hard earned and even Peter May was finding them in short supply in the last weeks of the season. In mid-summer two long-established batsmen, Fletcher and Eric Bedser, made way for young blood, as Ken Barrington and Micky Stewart took their places in the team, Stewart's presence especially sharpening the close fielding. For the last four matches of Surrey's triumphal march Raman was also excluded from the side, his final match for the county coming against Gloucestershire at Cheltenham.

His first full season with Surrey had brought Raman 836 runs at 26.96. For a man who had averaged over 50 the previous year it was a meagre return. A torn thigh muscle had not helped, but so far from aspiring to play Test cricket, he entertained no thoughts of a long-term future in the first-class game and had resolved to concentrate on finding a job away from cricket. His plan had been to look for a firm of chartered accountants with whom he could train with the aim of becoming a chartered secretary. Raman was making no secret of his intentions and this news reached the ears of Northants. As so often with players moving county, interest was the stronger for having seen ample evidence of Raman's talent when he had taken toll of their bowlers the previous summer. Raman recalls that the first approach came over a drink with Jock Livingston after play at the Oval. 'He said, "What are you going to do?" I said, "I'm going to give up the game at the end of the season. I want to get started on my accountancy training." So he said, "Why don't you come and play for us? If we can find you a firm of chartered accountants in Northampton, can you combine the two?"'

Surrey 1954

A Sandham (coach), PJ Loader, R Subba Row, EA Bedser, GAR Lock, TH Clark,
JC Laker, H Strudwick (scorer), S Tait (masseur)
B Constable, AJ McIntyre, PBH May, WS Surridge, AV Bedser, DGW Fletcher

This conversation was soon followed up by Dennis Brookes. A fine opening batsman of impeccable technique, unlucky to have played just one Test match, Brookes was in his first season as captain of the county. Though he had been a popular choice, for Northants it was a departure to have appointed a professional. Raman also recalls that Brookes, no doubt aware of the convention that county sides were led by amateurs, was quick to bring up what would later become a contentious issue. 'He said, "Well if you are going to come and join us, why don't you captain the side?"' Raman had demurred at concurring with any such presumption. 'I wouldn't have wanted to push him out in any way,' he remains at pains to stress. 'He was such a nice bloke.' A deal that would change the shape of Raman's life was formalised. 'They found me a delightful firm of accountants, A.C. Palmer. I was so lucky because it worked both ways. And without that slice of luck I would never have gone on and played for England.'

For many years Northants had lived with a Cinderella reputation. In the first three seasons after the War, led by amateurs with minimal playing credentials, the county had avoided bottom place in the Championship only once – in 1946 it had been the penultimate spot. Then, in 1949, came a change of outlook with the arrival of Freddie Brown, a captain who brought discipline and purpose as well as his own considerable all-round playing talent to a side long inured to failure. At the age of 38, he completed the double and, with few changes of personnel, led his team to sixth place. These giddy heights were not repeated, Northants ending the next four seasons tenth, thirteenth, eighth and eleventh. But no longer was the county chained to the bottom of the table and with some shrewd recruitment, notably of Jock Livingston, who in turn persuaded fellow Australian George Tribe to move across from the league, the side Brown was able to hand over to Dennis Brookes was significantly stronger than the one he had inherited. Brookes, the senior professional, had already covered extensively for Brown when his duties as a Test selector had restricted him to only 17 championship matches in 1953. Taking over full-time, he led his side to seventh place.

Whatever Brookes may have achieved, however, there was still a yearning around Northants to have an amateur as captain. In this they were merely conforming to an attitude widely seen in the committee rooms of other counties and fortified by the years of Freddie Brown. Whatever was said officially to Raman, the county's intentions were implicit: they looked upon him as a future captain. Surrey, already led by Stuart Surridge with May as heir apparent, could never have offered such an opening even if Raman had felt able to stay at the Oval. Moreover, with Stewart and Barrington starting to establish themselves as batsmen in 1954, Surrey could afford to raise no objection to Raman's special registration.

Raman moved into lodgings that Brookes had found close to his own home near the county ground, and his winter was spent working for A.C. Palmer. For his first summer with his new county Brookes retained the captaincy. It was seen as a chance for the new recruit to find his feet and observe, learning from one of the game's most experienced players. For both Raman and his new county there was a chastening start to the season. In their opening match against Yorkshire at Bradford, Northants were defeated in seven and a half hours on a rain-affected pitch, where their batsmen had no answer to the bowling of Bob Appleyard and Johnny Wardle. In a match where 40 wickets fell, Tribe, with nine for 45 in the second innings, gave Northants a glimpse of possible victory. They faced a target of 138, but Raman, who had made a duck in the first innings, was the only batsman to reach double figures as they fell 78 short. There was a better showing against Worcestershire, where Raman top scored with 80 in his first appearance in front of home supporters before rain consigned the match to a draw. Three drawn games were interspersed with three losses, to Middlesex, Hampshire and Sussex, as Northants had to wait until mid-June for their first win. It came at the expense of Nottinghamshire with Raman's 48 a welcome contribution in a lean period. A first century for his new county came fittingly in a well contested match at the Oval and it was followed by scores of 70 and 59 against the South African tourists, but the championship losses continued and by 8 July, with half their matches played, there had still been just one win and only Worcestershire lay below Northants in the table.

Sadly for Raman, no sooner had he found his form than he injured his hand when playing against Gloucestershire. Unable to bat in that match, he missed the next four, including welcome wins against Essex and Glamorgan, but returned against Middlesex at Lord's for a match lost by just 13 runs. A couple of scores in the twenties offered reassurance of his fitness but gave no indication of what was to come. Lancashire were the next visitors to Northampton on Saturday 23 July. Winning the toss, they reached 315 for eight and chose to bat on when the match resumed on Monday, allowing Malcolm Hilton to complete what would remain his only first-class century before declaring on 372 for nine. A solid reply was required and Northants batted with some enterprise to be 291 for four overnight with Raman undefeated on 116. Next day he progressed to 260 not out, an innings that occupied seven and three-quarter hours with 28 boundaries. It was the highest score of the first-class season and the highest ever for Northants. Yet it was still an innings played with team needs in mind. Only a partnership with Syd Starkie that went on to add 156, still standing as the county's ninth-wicket record at the end of the 2016 season, ensured first innings points in a match that had long been destined to end as a draw.

Perhaps this was the innings that Northants needed to inspire them. There were now six victories in a row to propel the county up to seventh place in the table, matching their performance of the previous year. Derbyshire, Leicestershire, Somerset, Essex and Worcestershire were all well beaten with Livingston, Barrick and Brookes each making a century before it was Raman's turn to star again in the toughest of the five fixtures. His first-innings 90 not out against Essex at Wellingborough kept the first innings deficit to manageable proportions before Livingston, with an unbeaten 172 led the way in a victory charge that saw Northants pass a target of 332 in 202 minutes with quarter of an hour to spare. Worcestershire were trounced by an innings and 51 runs at Stourbridge, then the cake was truly iced when Surrey, with May, Laker and Lock on Test duty, were beaten by six wickets at Northampton. The batting heroes now were Peter Arnold and Tribe. Raman contributed little with the bat but the six close catches he held, five of them off the bowling of Tribe, were the most he would ever take in a first-class match. Three drawn matches brought an uneven season to an end. Raman's batting had been inconsistent, but he stood second to Livingston in the averages and his occasionally used leg spin had brought him 14 wickets.

6

'We must have an amateur'

The captaincy saga

The master plan should now have swung into operation with Raman succeeding to the captaincy, but plans for him to take over then stalled. Raman had always believed that, as his father had come from India, he might be exempt from National Service. 'I didn't really know what was going to happen,' he says, 'but I hoped I was going to dodge it.' Nevertheless he received papers requiring him to serve his two years. He now harbours no regrets. 'It was very good for me,' he admits. Joining the RAF, he spent the first four months on the Isle of Man in an Officer Cadet Training Unit before being commissioned. A young man who followed him there was Ian MacLaurin, who very briefly served under the command of the recently commissioned Raman, and who would later become chairman of Tesco and follow in Raman's footsteps at the TCCB and, as Lord MacLaurin, turn cricket's governing body into the ECB.

From the Isle of Man Raman was posted to the RAF Training Centre at Bridgnorth in Shropshire, where he spent the remainder of his two years as a Pilot Officer responsible for the welfare of sixty or more recruits as they passed through. 'You grow up light years when you are responsible for so many people,' he says. 'I look back on it all now and think I was quite wrong not to have wanted to do it.' Raman found life as an officer very congenial, while his home posting, widely arranged in National Service for those who were capable sportsmen, ensured that he was freely available for RAF and Combined Services teams. Over his two summers in the RAF he managed to play just seven games for his county.

Returning in 1958, Raman looked forward to a full summer devoted to county cricket, but the captaincy had been a matter for discussion in committee. In Raman's absence Northants' fortunes had taken a dramatic turn for the better. Fourth in 1956, their best for 43 years, they had finished the 1957 season second in the Championship. Though 94 points behind an all-conquering Surrey side, it was, with 1912, the finest performance in Northants' history – with Brookes entitled to take the credit. Why would any county wish to depose so successful a leader? It is a question that only makes sense in the light of attitudes to social class still prevalent in the first-class game.

Across the counties class distinctions that stemmed from birth and education were still rife. Committee rooms had a superfluity of those with suitably plummy voices, men who were instinctively comfortable with a society that divided officers from other ranks. 'We must have an amateur' was the clarion call across the shires. Yet changing times meant that there were few 'gentlemen' with the means to take a whole summer away from a money-earning career. Between 1946 and 1958 only six of the counties – Derbyshire, Essex, Glamorgan, Hampshire, Surrey and Yorkshire – had always been led by an amateur. Middlesex, where Bill Edrich had changed status after the War, might be added to the list; but, for a short chaotic time, he shared duties with Denis Compton, always a professional.

Elsewhere finding an amateur had not been for want of trying, but it had often been an unequal task and there had been uneven levels of success. Gloucestershire, facing a void with Sir Derrick Bailey's retirement after 1952, filled it first with Jack Crapp then George Emmett, to be followed in 1959 by Tom Graveney. It came as news to Raman to hear in 2016 that the Gloucestershire minute book reveals his own name as one under consideration for an approach. But it was no real surprise: such speculative possibilities were part and parcel of the game with too few amateurs of class to go round. At Kent the tenure of Bill Murray-Wood, an amateur, had come to a premature end when the players could take no more and Doug Wright, the senior professional, was installed. Les Berry had done the job at Leicestershire in the first three post-war season only when all attempts to find an amateur had failed; so, after an interim season when Stuart Symington, an army officer enjoying a period of extended leave, stepped in, the county had been delighted to recruit Charles Palmer, hitherto teaching at Bromsgrove School. But for 1958, when Palmer had retired, a professional, Willie Watson was purposefully recruited. At Lancashire the treasurer's son, Jack Fallows, with leadership skills alone to commend him, had taken the reins in the first post-war season, handing on to Ken Cranston, a dentist who knew he could afford only a couple of seasons of fun, and thence to Nigel Howard, a former secretary's son; but in 1954 the county bowed to the inevitable and appointed Cyril Washbrook, their senior professional. Somerset had had an array of leaders from the eccentric to the incompetent until Maurice Tremlett, a professional, was installed in 1956. At Sussex there had been three seasons with James Langridge as skipper until normal service was resumed with a string of Cambridge Blues – Sheppard, Doggart, Marlar and, later on, Dexter. Warwickshire had found an inspirational leader when they made the mould-breaking appointment of a professional by choice rather than default and were repaid when Tom Dollery led his side to the

Championship in 1951; but when the mantle passed to Eric Hollies, he and the rest of the dressing room heaved a sigh of relief that it had been possible to lure Mike Smith to Edgbaston – an amateur again! Finally Worcestershire had succumbed to professional captaincy when Reg Perks was appointed in 1955, but were pleased to have Peter Richardson, an amateur of farming rather than public school stock, to succeed him.

The pattern of change makes clear that many professional captains must have felt aware that there would always be those on committees who would regard their appointment as something of a stop gap. So it was logical that Wright should step down in favour of Cowdrey at Kent, but Lancashire's choice of Bob Barber imposed an unwelcome skipper on a dressing room where the players had wished to see one of their own succeed Washbrook. A greater indignity came at Gloucestershire, where the appointment of the Etonian Tom Pugh cost the county the services of their leading batsman when Graveney left for Worcestershire. At Leicestershire the steady professional hand of Watson was not enough to quell the clamour for an amateur when a successor was required. The county's choice, David Kirby, fresh from having captained Cambridge University, had given every indication that he would struggle for success in the first-class game – and he did. Even at Yorkshire, where Vic Wilson took office as the first professional captain in 1960, the previous appointment, to sort out an unruly dressing room, had been Ronnie Burnet, a man bereft of first-class playing credentials but quintessentially an amateur. The success of this move prompted Lancashire to turn to a man they believed to have a similar profile. Joe Blackledge was appointed to succeed Barber in 1962, but so far from matching Burnet, he led Lancashire to their lowest ever position, only the ineptness of Kirby's Leicestershire depriving them of the wooden spoon.

This, then, was the wider background to Northants' wish to revert to an amateur captain. However, it took little note of the prevailing feeling in the dressing room, where attitudes were moulded less by any antipathy to Raman than by an almost reverential attachment to Brookes. 'A wonderful captain,' says Peter Arnold. 'Most of us felt that, given one more year, we'd have got that first place or made a very good challenge.' Peter talks of Brookes' insight into the game, recalling his own debut innings in championship cricket. Playing at Old Trafford in 1951, he went in just after Brian Statham, with the second new ball, had broken through. First Statham bowled Norman Oldfield, who had just completed his hundred. Next ball, Vince Broderick also saw his wicket shattered. Peter was facing a hat trick. 'As I was picking up my bat, Dennis said to me, "You won't see the ball. You can take your right hand off the bat. Because the ball will be in the blockhole." So I get out there and take guard. Statham comes up and bowls, and it goes off the inside edge of my bat down to fine leg. And that ball was exactly what Dennis had said it would be.'

In later seasons, when he and Brookes regularly opened together, Peter came to admire his partner's understanding of the pace on a ball as they ran their singles. 'We pinched runs left, right and centre.' This same cricketing judgement was seen in Brookes' captaincy. 'He knew every player that we played against inside out. And he would set the field accordingly, and he would change the bowling accordingly.' Brookes also earned a reputation for his understanding of the pace of a game – judging the timing of his declarations and knowing when to dangle a carrot.

On a personal level the players had happily accepted Raman, his amateur background of little consequence to them. But wherever he has gone in life, he has invariably been recalled as a quietly charming personality rather than a life and soul of the party type, and he had held his distance from the drinking crowd at close of play. Raman was also disadvantaged by his age. Only 23 when he arrived, he was many years younger than the old guard in the team, while his background and education would have sheltered him from the rough and tumble ethos of a dressing room where some strong personalities abounded. A small county, Northants had thrived through the recruitment of Australians from the leagues, and when regulations made it less practical to sign players from around the dominions, a pioneering secretary Ken Turner focussed his attention on acquiring the most promising products of the minor counties, with the north-east always well represented. A bar in the 1950s, as recalled by Peter Arnold, with Jack Manning insisting on buying the drinks and then 'You couldn't lend me a fiver, could you?' was hardly the atmosphere where Raman would have felt at home.

Whatever the views of the Northants players, there had also been voices off the field pressing for Brookes to remain. Nor had it always been a simple choice between him and Raman. Minutes from 1956 bring the name of 'Pom Pom' Fellows-Smith into the mix. A three-year Blue at Oxford, he had averaged 28 with the bat for the University, while the 53 wickets he had taken had come at almost 37 each. His one season for Northants came the next year, 1957, when he started in the second eleven before a run in the first team began with some impressive scores but tailed off without improving his career average, while he took not a single wicket in 12 championship matches. Concerns expressed that he might not be quite good enough as a player seemed to be confirmed, notwithstanding that he would play four Test matches for his native South Africa in 1960. Raman, by contrast, was seen as 'a class player'. His cause had been championed by Freddie Brown and it was supported by Rawlins Hawtin, a long-serving chairman of the club and now chairman of selectors. They had seen the good sense in his having one year playing under Brookes, but now felt it best to make the switch while he would still have the wise counsel of the former captain available to him. A committee minute from 1956 had already recorded that Brookes was prepared to play under Raman, as Raman remembers him making clear from the outset, but the subsequent on-field success became a complicating factor. Leading the faction who maintained that it would be foolish and unfair to Brookes to expect him to step down was the powerful figure of George Vials. 'Tubby' Vials had captained the county from 1911 to 1913 and, having played a prominent part on the committee, succeeded to the presidency in 1957. He was recorded as saying it would be a blunder for Raman to accept an offer of the captaincy.

It wasn't an easy matter: the county wanted to keep both players, for their potential runs if nothing else. Moreover, apart from Brookes' initial presumption back in 1954 that Raman would be appointed in due course, there had always been at least a strong inference in committee circles that Raman was pencilled in to take on the captaincy. In a world of nods and winks the appointment would always have needed endorsement by the committee, and in keeping with the conspiratorial atmosphere it is instructive to see a formal minute that it had seemed better to speak to Raman rather than write. Had Raman not taken over at this point, he could justifiably have felt that he had been lured to Northampton under false pretences. In all this the good sense of Dennis Brookes cannot be underestimated. From his early days in the 1930s he had come to understand how these things were done and he had learned to accept them. Put crudely, and though Brookes was destined to become Chairman of the Magistrates' Bench in Northampton, he knew his station in life. A naturally kind and gentle man, he gave Raman his full support and did what he could to quell any opposition, though the words of wicket-keeper Keith Andrew suggest he may not have been wholly successful. 'I'm afraid that some of the players didn't support him to the degree that they supported Dennis.' Whatever Brookes may have said, there were those among the senior players whose view would never change. As Andrew put it: 'Raman was a very pleasant bloke. But he didn't have the knowledge and experience that Dennis did, and he wasn't a natural leader like Freddie Brown.' Peter Arnold's view remains that it was a pity Brookes was not given just one more year to strive for that still elusive championship with Raman waiting until 1959 to take over.

7

'Into the top flight of English batsmen'

Test match debut

By taking over a team that had come second in the Championship, Raman stepped into a hot seat. Only if the county managed to displace Surrey would supporters be satisfied. Raman had the same players at his command as Brookes with one crucial exception – there would be no Livingston. In his eight seasons with Northants the aggressive Australian left-hander had scored more than 13,000 runs at an average of over 45, but in 1957 he had been hampered by a knee injury and, with his form suffering, he had decided to retire at the age of 37. Raman would hope for his own contribution to replace Livingston's runs in a batting line-up, where Brookes, at 42, was still a fine player with an established opening partner in Peter Arnold. To follow would

Dennis Brookes and Jock Livingston

be Brian Reynolds, a local man, a battler who made many of his runs when the going was toughest, and Des Barrick, a jovial team-mate whose ever-present nerves would be relieved by incessant chattering. In the middle order George Tribe had always proved himself good for the thousand runs that would eventually bring him seven doubles in eight seasons.

To spearhead the attack was Frank Tyson, a bowler whose sheer speed always gave his captain a weapon other counties could never hope to match. He was to enjoy a good enough season to merit a return trip to Australia, though he was no longer quite the force he had once been. There was little to complement the pace of Tyson, the new ball generally being taken by a young Albert Lightfoot, who was destined to have a more productive season as a batsman. However, it was in spin that the county's great strength lay. Though the regular attack comprised three who all bowled with the left arm, they still offered plenty of variety. The match winner was Tribe with his back of the hand style that few county batsmen could confidently read. Jack Manning, more the pace of Derek Underwood, moved the ball in the air, while Mick Allen was a more orthodox spinner. Completing the regular eleven, Keith Andrew would be awaiting the stumping chances the spinners would bring.

The summer was to prove one of the most dismal on record for its almost incessant rain. No fewer than 23 championship matches were abandoned without a decision on first innings, five of them, rather more than their share, involving Northants. With pitches still uncovered, runs were hard-earned. The average per wicket, 21.13, was, with just one exception, the lowest since the First World War, but it brought with it the compensation of many matches completed in reduced hours simply because of the dominance of ball over bat. Moreover, the points system provided every incentive to risk all for a win, which brought 12 points. Only two points were available in lost or drawn games, but a side could only win these if, at the point of gaining a first innings lead, they had the faster scoring rate, while a winning side could increase the reward to 14 if posting a first innings lead at a faster rate.

The season began with a disappointing loss to Glamorgan, but the first two victories owed much to Raman's enterprise. There was a three-wicket win at Leicester, where he closed the Northants innings 66 behind and was rewarded by a challenge to score 225 at 80 an hour to win the match. Raman's own 70 not out brought the winning hit from the fourth ball of the final over. Then there was a 48-run victory over Derbyshire at Northampton when Raman, in the manner typical of Stuart Surridge, declared the second innings at 68 for seven. Northants' batsmen had run to the wicket as they took just 35 minutes to set the visitors a target of 146 in 130 minutes, after which the three spinners finished the job on a drying pitch with 20 minutes to spare.

This was the fifth match of a season that had already brought Raman four fifties, and Northants were in good heart as they travelled to the Oval to meet a Surrey side that had opened with five championship wins but were now deprived of their Test players. A century from Micky Stewart was the cornerstone of a sound batting performance as Surrey carried on into the second day, declaring at 378 for five. If the Northants batsmen believed that an attack shorn of Laker, Lock and Loader, and with Alec Bedser unfit, might offer easy pickings, they were soon to be disillusioned. At 18 for three, when Raman came in to bat, Dave Sydenham had despatched Brookes, Arnold and Reynolds without the assistance of fielders. Raman and Barrick added 71, but at 95 for five Barrick and Tribe had both been dismissed. As Albert Lightfoot joined Raman, the follow-on loomed. By close of play, it had been averted. When their stand ended, they had been together for six and three-quarter hours. They had added 376, still a county record for the sixth wicket and, at the time, the best for any Northants wicket. For Lightfoot his 119 was his maiden first-class century.

Raman had dominated the stand. When he was bowled by Tom Clark he had made 300, the highest score of the first-class season and the first triple century in English cricket for eight years. At the time it was the highest individual score for Northants, surpassing his own record set three years earlier. Raman had batted 566 minutes and hit 42 fours. His innings had come in one of the few matches where the bat held dominance in this wretched summer. The inevitable draw was the first time Surrey had ceded points to any opponent that summer. With 74 points from seven matches, they still headed the table comfortably, while Northants lay eighth with 30 from six. The gap would soon close.

For Raman there were further fine innings. At Old Trafford he scored exactly 100 in a match where not even the two first innings were completed, then he took 110 off the Gloucestershire bowlers at Northampton in yet another rain-affected draw. Rain ensured that there was no decision in the match with Sussex, and it continued to shape the destiny of the Championship when a blank first day against Yorkshire at Northampton ensured a bowler's wicket once the sun came out. Brian Close made 46 of his side's 67 before Raman top-scored with 21 in Northants' 107 to give his side a lead that was to prove decisive as a pitch recovering from a thunderstorm gave Yorkshire's batsmen no respite at their second attempt. This time they succumbed for 65, Tribe ending with match figures of 15 for 31, still the best ever recorded for Northants.

Nottinghamshire, destined to end at the foot of the table, now secured one of only three wins they would achieve all summer. It came after Raman had chosen to bat first on a soft pitch and seen his side bowled out for 94, a position from which they never recovered. This was the last disappointment before a run of six consecutive victories. Raman was still in the runs as Northants came out on top in close matches away to Gloucestershire and Somerset. He missed the ten wicket win in the return match with Notts, but was back for the innings defeat of Kent before handing over to Brookes for the last two games of the winning run – an 11 run nail-biter in the penultimate over against Warwickshire at Edgbaston and a four-wicket victory at home to Worcestershire after Tribe had taken nine for 43 in their second innings.

With 140 points from 19 matches, Northants now stood second not to Surrey (134 from 19), who had gone off the boil, but to Hampshire (152 from 18). But where was Raman as Northants surged towards the top? On the first occasion he was engaged at Lord's doing battle for the Gentlemen against the Players. In a summer in which only four batsmen averaged over 40, Raman had taken the eyes of the England selectors, who invariably picked the two sides with a view to looking at Test candidates. 'If Subba Row has a strong claim to go to Australia, now is the time for him to take it,' wrote John Woodcock in *The Times*. It was a message that did not fall on deaf ears: from his team's innings of 219 for eight, Raman, coming in at the fall of the first wicket, made an undefeated 102 in just under four hours against an attack led by Fred Trueman and Brian Statham with Johnny Wardle in support, enabling Woodcock to write that he had 'shown the most splendid determination while lifting himself into the top flight of English batsmen.'

Adding an undefeated 44 in the second innings, Raman's dogged batting in front of a discerning Lord's crowd had booked him a place in the England team for the fourth Test, which was announced two days after the match. As happened in those days, the names of those chosen reached the players at the same time as the general public, and Raman still recalls the thrill of hearing his own name announced on the radio as he was taking part in a club match at New Malden. 'I couldn't believe it,' he says. A weak New Zealand side had put up little resistance in the first three encounters of the summer and, facing the need to choose their side to tour Australia, the selectors had rested Cowdrey, Bailey and Laker giving first caps to Cambridge captain Ted Dexter and Ray Illingworth alongside Raman. So, as Brookes took back the reins at Northants, Raman made for Old Trafford.

Following scores of 94, 137, 47, 74, 67 and 129 New Zealand, after winning the toss, now got rather more of the grit between their teeth in battling their way to 267 against an attack of Trueman, Statham, Lock and Illingworth. It took them nine and three quarter hours, but England domination was soon restored with an opening partnership of 126 between Peter Richardson and

Willie Watson, and there was little relief when Richardson was replaced by May, who was soon into his stride and on the way to his tenth Test hundred. When bad light stopped play on the second day England had reached 192 for two. The third day, a Saturday, was curtailed by rain after an already damp and damaged pitch had been subjected to special repairs, permitted under the regulations of the time, to the area in front of the left-handers' off stump. The captains had also, more controversially, agreed to allow the covers to be extended over the repaired area.

When play eventually resumed, Tom Graveney was immediately caught at slip and Raman made his way to the pitch with its makeshift repairs. Further rain ensured that it would be a short stay, proceedings being brought to a halt at 206 for three. The timing was fortuitous: it meant that Raman's wicket was still intact as the selectors sat down on the Sunday to choose their team for the winter tour. His CV was illuminated by his performances for the Gentlemen, not by the disappointing end to his innings for only 9 on a rain-shortened Monday. He had batted 67 minutes, adding 55 with his captain, but his place on the boat to Australia was already secure. The selectors had decided against taking Dexter, who now came in on a difficult pitch and hit the ball with the power of a kicking horse, his 52 coming in 87 minutes with two sixes. Had the touring party been chosen 24 hours later, the popular press opined, it might have included 'Lord Ted' in preference to the less charismatic Subba Row! For R.C. Robertson-Glasgow Dexter's omission was 'the biggest clanger I have ever known selectors anywhere to commit.'

The aggression of Dexter and May, who hit four sixes, enabled lost time to be made up. Though New Zealand began the final day on 30 for no wicket, there was no respite for their batsmen whose innings occupied 52 overs before the last wicket fell at 85 to give England their fourth decisive win of the series, this time by an innings and 13 runs.

It was time now for Raman to return to Northants and continue the push for the championship title. Sadly, his season had already peaked as had that of his county. The run of six victories was followed by successive losses to Essex, Leicestershire, by just 20 runs, and Worcestershire. There was some respite with a draw in the return match with Essex, but it was followed by a further loss to Kent at Dover, where enterprising declarations saw Northants finally undone on a drying pitch. The three draws that followed were all rain-affected with only the Hampshire match at Southampton offering any prospect of a result. By this stage Northants' hopes of the title had long faded, but, while Surrey had recovered their best form, Hampshire still held realistic hopes of unseating them. Raman set up a cliff-hanger. His carrot, challenging Hampshire to score 170 in two hours, ended with the last pair at the crease needing six more runs. There was a watery draw with Middlesex at Lord's and it was scant consolation to close the season with a victory against Glamorgan at Ebbw Vale.

Though Raman ended with only May, Watson and Mike Smith ahead of him in the season's averages, his form had dipped in the closing weeks. Until he hit an unbeaten 115 in the final match he had not passed fifty since his return from England duty. In a side so strong in spin he bowled only 15 overs, though he did prise out the final two wickets of the season just when the Glamorgan tail was proving an irritant. But what of his captaincy? In the anodyne prose of *Wisden*, 'he led the side capably,' but though he had closed the gap behind Surrey from 94 points to 52, ending in fourth place meant that he had presided over a season of disappointment. There were occasions when he had kept games alive with daring declarations, but the county were to do no better in the seasons that lay ahead and, in the eyes of Keith Andrew, Raman remained a Surrey player at heart, perhaps lacking northern grit: 'He wanted to play brighter cricket and he tried to keep the traditions of cricket at the forefront. But sometimes we'd be 150 for six at lunchtime and you don't win matches that way.'

8

'A Bennett's type fracture'

Disappointments in Australia

A letter from Raman's dentist in Croydon lodged in MCC's files at Lord's certifies that an inspection on 15 September had found his teeth in good order. This was one of the small precautions taken to minimise the risk of health problems with the 16 players. The formalities of the day included a letter to each player's county: 'I am directed by the MCC Committee to ask your Committee if they will allow......to tour Australia this winter.' Shades of Lord Hawke withholding such permission! Preserved also in the tour file at Lord's are the contracts that Raman and others signed over a sixpenny stamp, making as clear as legal language can that they were expected to do as they were told and to behave as Trappist monks should they encounter anyone from the press. For professionals the tour fee was £750 with the chance to earn a bonus of £150. What the amateurs earned as compensation for loss of earnings was a matter of growing concern elsewhere around Lord's, but they, like the professionals, were to receive £7 a week in expenses towards such incidentals as tips, taxis and toiletries, a sum which it was hoped would be modest enough to keep the Inland Revenue at bay.

Lengthy correspondence reveals how long the trip had been in the planning. Concerned for players' family lives, MCC had pleaded successfully for a reduction in the country matches; but a request for the New Zealand leg to be sandwiched into the middle weeks of the main tour was firmly rejected by the Australian Board. Letters seeking agreement over the covering of pitches and times of the tea interval were matched in importance by requests from state governors for formal receptions at each port of call around the country. The players, it was later reported, preferred drinks parties to more formal dinners – and they would not be short of such entertainment. 'We weren't too keen on stuffy dinners, much preferred to be having a drink with one's pals,' Raman agrees.

The party that embarked the *SS Iberia* on 20 September did so with a reputation as the strongest team in the world. The Ashes had been held since 1953 and the past four summers had seen Test series won, many of the matches by embarrassingly emphatic margins. There had been a blip in South Africa, where the series had only been drawn after England had been two up, but there remained an enviable choice of pace bowlers – Trueman, Statham,

Tyson and Loader – with Laker supreme as the world's best off spinner in an attack complemented by the left-arm spin of his Surrey colleague Lock or Wardle, whose back of the hand variety tended to give him the edge overseas. Bailey was an all-rounder whose obduracy had saved matches with bat and ball, while Evans' ebullience and skill assured the very best support behind the stumps. The batting was of less certain quality, but the class of May, Cowdrey and Graveney was unquestioned, while Richardson had made an impressive start to his Test career as an opener.

Yet before long everything was starting to go wrong. Wardle's spat with Yorkshire ultimately ruled him out of the party to be replaced only some weeks into the tour by John Mortimore, whose credentials were more modest, while commentators easily overlooked the unproven nature of the support batting. Milton had opened his Test career with a century, but it was against a limited New Zealand attack, while Watson was chosen, at the age of 38, on the back of an excellent summer, but the two centuries from his earlier Test career had to be set against many occasions when he had disappointed. The other reserve batsman was Raman with a single Test cap.

Before long the tour would be embroiled in controversy over the legality of the actions of several Australian bowlers and the poor quality of the home umpires, but before this lay what would be the last journey to Australia that a touring team from England would make wholly by sea. For Raman it was the beginning of six months of sunshine and good companionship, whatever his misfortunes off the field. His passion for bridge found others for ever willing to make up a four. It was not untrammelled success, *The Times* reporting that he and Bailey 'arrived on one occasion at six hearts more by instinct than convention, only to find themselves four down, doubled and vulnerable.' However, the report added, they were many thousands of points ahead of Watson and Graveney.

A short stop at Aden provided a chance to visit the bazaars and enjoy a few drinks at Government House before the *Iberia* sailed on to Bombay. Now began the on-field frustrations that would dog Raman's tour. While their ship tied up for a few days, the whole party flew to Colombo, where an eagerly awaited pair of one-day matches were scheduled. In the first, Raman was one of the eleven who got onto the field for just 28 overs as the local batsmen reached 47 for six. Rain then halted proceedings and ensured that there would be no play against the President's XI in the match planned for the following day.

The party arrived at Fremantle on 13 October, four days ahead of their first match. Even before reaching Bombay MCC had been beset by injury when

MCC team to Australia and New Zealand, 1958/59

R Swetman, CA Milton, FS Trueman, PJ Loader, W Watson, JB Mortimore, PE Richardson
G Duckworth (scorer), JB Statham, GAR Lock, ER Dexter, R Subba Row,
TW Graveney, FH Tyson, D Montague (masseur)
FR Brown (manager), TE Bailey, MC Cowdrey, PBH May, TG Evans,
JC Laker, EDR Eagar (assistant manager)

Watson, in rising from a deck chair, had damaged his knee so badly that it required an operation in Australia. His absence from the first six matches of the tour gave Raman extra incentive to stake a place in the Test side. Omitted from the first match against Western Australia at Perth, he made only 14 and 15 against a Combined XI. May, Cowdrey and Graveney had all played big innings in the early matches, but Richardson and Milton, the opening pair, had done no better than Raman. They recovered form against South Australia, where Raman, at No. 4, was again dismissed in the teens, scoring just 17 as MCC recorded their first win of the tour. For John Woodcock in *The Times* the paucity of leg spinners in England was now causing problems to some of MCC's batsmen and, with Raman and Milton, 'it was harrowing to watch them searching for an answer to it.'

Moving on to Melbourne, Raman played what was to be his highest innings of the tour with a much needed 83 in the defeat of Victoria by 87 runs. On the huge Melbourne ground he managed only two boundaries, but his innings was full of characteristic nudges and a partnership of 164 with Milton was notable for the pair's smart running between the wickets. The match was ultimately won in dramatic fashion as Lock captured the last two wickets with the sixth and seventh balls of the final eight-ball over. Milton's century advanced his case for a place for the Tests that were approaching, and it was further strengthened when he and Richardson added 170 in the second innings of the next match as MCC, required to follow on, were staring at defeat against New South Wales. Raman had sat out this match, but against an Australian XI he followed a first-innings duck with an undefeated 68 in the second innings, a 'workmanlike' contribution to a stand of 180 with May. May's knee had been a cause of concern, but a century in each innings of the match suggested that there was little wrong with it. With a pitch that aided their spinners, MCC won by 345 runs, their most impressive performance of the tour.

For the Queensland match at Brisbane, the last game before the first Test, Watson made his first appearance of the tour. He made single figure scores in both innings, but Raman took the chance to show that he was finding form with 51, top score in a disappointing MCC total of 151. Rain eventually condemned the match to a draw, but not before fate had dealt the cruellest of blows to Raman. 'I was fielding in the gully and the ball was slashed towards me. I didn't see it and it hit me right here and when I looked at my thumb it was hanging down. I tried to put it back, but I couldn't.' Raman spent the night in a Brisbane hospital, where the hand was operated on. The surgeon's medical report identified 'a Bennett's type fracture at the base of the first right metacarpal.' This formal diagnosis came in a letter dated 3 December that went on to say that Raman 'should be fit to resume full cricketing activities in approximately twelve (12) days from this date.'

Though there were reports of gentle practice in early January, it would be 44 days before Raman played his next match. In the meantime three Test matches had been played and the Ashes hung by a thread. Moreover, Raman's injury had triggered the decision to call for another batsman, and Ted Dexter was now with the party. Had Raman remained fit and had he been regarded as a possible opener, a Test place might have been his. But, while his thumb healed, he could only watch as the failures of his team-mates multiplied. Richardson and Milton had no success in the first Test. Milton then broke a finger and missed the second Test, so Bailey was moved up to open, while Watson came in at number three. Richardson failed again and was dropped for the third Test, allowing Milton, whose finger had just mended, to partner Bailey. Dexter, though having shown no form, was preferred to Watson.

Australia had won the first two Tests, both by the comfortable margin of eight wickets, while the third had ended in a draw only after May and Cowdrey had mounted a recovery from a first innings deficit of 138. Over the three matches the vulnerability of the batting had been remorselessly exposed with the opening partnerships worth 16, 28, 7, 3, 19 and 30. To retain the Ashes nothing less than victory in both the remaining Tests would now do.

Raman's return came in the second match against Victoria. With bush fires raging in the countryside and the mercury reaching 109F in the shade at the ground, some of MCC's fielders had ice cubes inside their panama hats, and the fast bowlers were restricted to short spells as the home batsmen reached 286. Those auditioning for places in the Test side then fared poorly: with 31 on the board, Raman had joined Richardson, Milton and Dexter back in the shade of the pavilion. Cowdrey, captaining the side in the absence of May, then joined forces with Watson, whose 141 was to be his most substantial innings of the tour. Their stand of 169 enabled MCC to gain a lead on first innings and, when 154 were required to win, Richardson and Milton provided a sound platform and victory was achieved by nine wickets, but not before Milton had had to retire with his finger broken once again.

If Milton's injury, which ended his tour, had opened a place in the Test team, Watson had certainly booked it, and when Raman managed only 24 in a rain-spoilt game with New South Wales, his case for inclusion had not been strengthened. The fourth Test ended in a further emphatic defeat, by ten wickets, but it had seen England's only opening partnership of substance, when Watson helped Richardson add 89 in the second innings. Three one-day matches were played before a demoralised team returned to Melbourne to end their time in Australia with a further loss in the fifth Test, this time by nine wickets.

Injuries sustained in a car accident had ruled out Statham and Loader from this final match in Australia and they, together with Milton, Bailey, Laker and Evans, missed the New Zealand leg of the tour, for which it had been intended to take 14 players. The twelve who travelled comprised the team from the fifth Test minus Bailey but plus Raman and Mortimore. For Raman there were three provincial matches, but he was left carrying the drinks for the two Test matches, the only player in a party that had grown to 18 not to play in a Test match.

The manager's report on the tour made plain that the standard of umpiring had been poor and this had compounded the problem of suspect actions which was plaguing Australian cricket. To E.W. Swanton there had never been such a blatant instance of throwing as Meckiff, while fast bowlers had also been permitted to drag their back leg to an such an extent that Rorke, 'three and a half feet over the batting crease' in the official report, was able to deliver the ball from as close as 18 yards to the batsman. The latter problem was soon to be addressed by making the landing of the front foot the critical determinant in calling no balls, but the elimination of doubtful actions was to remain a continuing saga that would soon see the South African Geoff Griffin exiled from the game, and it would rumble on to the present day collecting its victims from every decade.

Most of the hotels in which the team had stayed were felt to have come up to muster, the manager reported, though the charges for dinners at 25 to 35 shillings (£1.25 to £1.75) were considered so excessive that players had been allowed a guinea (£1.05) to eat out. Brown commented that such was the desire of most hoteliers to have the team stay in their establishments that some effort might be made to strike special deals for accommodating future parties. Such an oversight in tour planning perhaps typified some of MCC's less than commercial ways of working that Raman would soon be questioning, when his later career was to take him into the heart of cricket administration.

Notwithstanding Brown's embarkation warning to Trueman, as reported by Tom Graveney – 'One false step from you and you'll be on the first boat home', the conduct of all members of the party had been exemplary. 'One of the best behaved and quietest living teams that MCC have ever sent abroad, and they were most popular wherever they went.'

After playing in ten first-class matches Raman's batting average was 34.50. Only May, Graveney and Cowdrey were above him. His captain and good friend Peter May had this to say of his contribution to the tour: 'A disappointment to me, but, again, injury to his hand came at a time when he might have settled down. The bounce of the leg spinners was always a great problem to his batting, and he does not really play straight enough to be successful on the faster Australian wickets. He is rather laboured in the field, though he is a safe catcher near the wicket. A delightful person to have on an MCC tour.'

9

'A sure anchor with a habit of making runs'

A summer of consolidation

If 1958 will always be remembered as one of the wettest of all British summers, 1959 was in sharp contrast. Endless days of sunshine in the second half of the summer made it an arduous season for bowlers with championship runs per wicket, at 26.88, the highest of the decade. Also contributing to a difficult time for traditional finger spinners was a new regulation that pitches could be wholly covered overnight and once play had been called off for the day. For Raman, as captain of Northants, it meant that the principal weapons in his attack, the left-arm spinners, were blunted. Though Tribe had his back of the hand variety, he, Manning and Allen were less effective as a trio than in previous years, Allen before long making way for the leg spin of a young Peter Watts. For nine championship matches Northants were without Tyson and in his absence there was a limp pace attack. Contributing to a difficult year was a batting line-up that did not really cash in on the hard pitches that saw no fewer than 23 batsmen across the country pass 2,000 first-class runs. A broken leg sustained playing football kept Brian Reynolds out of action all season.

With Tribe and Brookes entering their final seasons, this was seen as a last chance to bid for the title before an inevitable period of rebuilding. It started disappointingly at Derby, where Raman's undefeated 127 in a total of 210 came after his side had been 49 for seven. Another poor batting display in the second innings left Derbyshire too little to do and the match was lost by four wickets. Raman missed the first home fixture, a loss by eight wickets to Lancashire, but he was again the mainstay of the batting with 117 not out in a ten-wicket defeat of Warwickshire. Two close matches were then lost. After three declarations Somerset edged to victory by two wickets with three minutes to spare, then Essex squeezed home by two runs at Ilford with only one minute remaining, Northants' last three wickets having fallen at the same score. Raman's good early season form had continued in this match. After contributing 97 to a first innings total of 193, his 49 was the major contribution to a partnership with Brookes, whose own 107 might have got Northants home had he not been run out as the asking rate demanded risks. When a nine-wicket win against Leicestershire came early on the third day, it was only the second victory to set against four matches lost.

If it had been a dispiriting start, Raman had shown himself willing to play his part in setting up the close finishes in which Northants had ended just the wrong side of the winning post. Perhaps he felt the need to be more cautious in taking on Yorkshire at Headingley. His own prime form with the bat continued with 126 not out in the second innings. This came after defeat had seemed likely at 77 for seven, but Keith Andrew helped add 124 before a declaration that asked Yorkshire to score 271 in 190 minutes, an invitation that was declined. Mick Norman still goes into raptures about Raman's inning that day: 'The rest of us totally floundered. I can't imagine anyone else doing it. He showed us how to play.'

Raman's fourth century of the season came at Cardiff in early June in yet another match characterised by declarations. This time he hit exactly 100 in a total of 243 for eight. After rain interventions, Raman's challenge to Glamorgan was to make 231 at 72 an hour, a target the home side reached with six minutes in hand. Had Raman once again been just too generous? A second win against Leicestershire, one of the weaker counties, came at Hinckley by the comfortable margin of nine wickets with much owed to 154 from Brookes. But when Middlesex came to Northampton, only first innings points were taken after Raman's declaration now proved too conservative to tempt the visitors' batsmen. With ten of their 28 matches played, thoughts of a championship title had long become a fading dream: Northants were now eleventh in the table.

Nottinghamshire, who would end bottom of the Championship, proved easy meat in the next match. An innings win was followed by another of the many cliffhangers of Northants' season. This time what had once looked an almost certain victory over Essex ended with Northants' ninth wicket pair together and eight required from the final over. With two still needed off the last ball, Gordon Williamson was run out. Sixties against both Notts and Essex confirmed Raman's fine form, and he may have been unlucky not to have received a call from the national selectors, though he had not helped his cause in an early season match for MCC against Yorkshire at Lord's, when England's need to rebuild after the disastrous Ashes tour had prompted a look at some fresh faces.

By mid-summer the struggle was on to find an opening pair for England. Arthur Milton and Ken Taylor had failed in the first two Tests and newspapers were able to headline that a pair of GPs had been called to the rescue – Geoff Pullar winning a first cap alongside Gilbert Parkhouse, recalled after eight years. *The Times* speculated that there might have been other solutions: 'The temptation must have been to revert to Cowdrey or prevail upon Subba Row, who is a fine player of fast bowling, to step into the breach. It was known, however, that this appeals to neither player.' Raman reflects on this assessment, mindful that for most of his career, even when he was opening regularly for England, he chose to bat lower down when he returned to Northants. 'I enjoyed opening,' he says, 'I didn't mind quick bowling, even if it was very quick. You get used to it after a time. But I was brought up to bat lower down. I wasn't brought up as an opener. But later on I got an opportunity to open and you don't turn that sort of thing down.' As with Cowdrey, to Raman going in first was 'not my natural choice.'

Raman leads out the Northants team against Kent at Kettering, 1959

A fifty from Raman at Kettering helped in the defeat of Kent, after which there was much disapproval from the crowd at Worcester when the normally enterprising Northants batsmen refused to be tempted by a target of 293 in three hours and 20 minutes, Raman himself spending two hours over an undefeated 13 that led to booing on his return to the pavilion. Against Gloucestershire at Peterborough heavy rain turned the outground pitch into one of which spin bowlers can seldom do more than dream, enabling Manning to record a career best of eight for 43; but the visitors' three spinners, David Allen, John Mortimore and Sam Cook, had the final say, taking their side to victory by 50 runs in a low-scoring match.

There was yet another tense draw at Trent Bridge where Northants, with one wicket left, were four runs short, but Raman was not there to see it, with

Tribe captaining the side in his absence. In accordance with the priorities of the day, Raman was representing the Gentlemen at Lord's, where Dennis Brookes was paid the honour of leading the Players. The selectors' concern to find openers saw Raman cast in this unfamiliar role in partnership with Bob Barber. Getting his head down in the second innings, he contributed 55 to a stand of 173 for the second wicket with Mike Smith, which enabled the Gentlemen to avert defeat after a first innings deficit of 171.

Back with his county, Raman remained in the middle order for the next few games, as Somerset just beat the clock to win by four wickets at Taunton, Northants got the better of a draw against Surrey and Yorkshire, destined to be champions this year, were trounced by an innings and 144 runs. This was the occasion of Raman's highest score of the season, his 183 not out coming in sunshine on the Saturday, after which a thunderstorm gave the Northants bowlers a pitch on which Tyson and Lightfoot held all the cards as Yorkshire could muster no more than 64 in their second innings. Another hundred for Raman at Bristol, this time in the second innings, set up the prospect of another Northants win, but once again, with a crucial catch dropped, the fates decreed that Gloucestershire should squeeze home by two wickets.

Raman now decided to open the batting. Brookes, having had a lean time, dropped down the order, while Arnold was left out of the side. So Raman partnered Mick Norman in a drawn match against Warwickshire, the new arrangement immediately bringing Norman his maiden first-class century though it put a brake on Raman's flow of runs. *Wisden* nevertheless considered this pairing the side's most successful. There was 62 for Raman in the second innings against Hampshire in another match narrowly lost, this time by two wickets. The England selectors, patently more in need of an opener than another middle-order batsman in the Test side, were no doubt pleased to see Raman going in at number one, but he recalls no request for him to do so.

An injury kept Raman out of a drawn match against Worcestershire, but he returned to play against Kent at Dover, though contributing little as Northants, bowled out for 80 and 86, were defeated by 134 runs. Raman had scored only 139 runs in six innings since promoting himself, but earlier deeds may have persuaded the selectors that he was their man once Parkhouse had laboured over his runs at Old Trafford. For the final Test at the Oval Raman was chosen to partner Pullar. In a series where India had already lost the first four matches comprehensively, their batsmen now laboured for five hours in making 140 on a good batting pitch. Trueman with four for 24 was their chief destroyer, while leg-spinner Tommy Greenhough was allowed to bowl 29 overs for 36 runs. With 15 overs to begin their reply, the two left-handers reached 35 without being parted. Pullar was out early next morning, soon to be followed by Cowdrey. This brought together Raman and Mike Smith. With Smith in prime form and with a hundred under his belt from the previous Test, the pair added 169, at the time a record for England's third wicket against India. As when they had batted for the Gentlemen, Smith's dominance was in contrast to a more laboured innings from his partner, prompting John Woodcock in *The Times* to describe Raman as 'a journeyman by comparison' before going on to sum up his batting virtues in words that echo the sentiments of his contemporaries: 'No-one could say he made batting look easy. That is something he does only when his timing is working perfectly, and now he was playing for his place as an opening batsman in West Indies. He showed what we know already, that he is a sure anchor with a habit of making runs. It is part of his secret that he plays within his limitations, always waiting for the ball he fancies and seldom getting himself out.'

The description is hardly poetic, but for Woodcock this was the way to lay a foundation, something that he had seen all too infrequently for England since the days of Hutton and Washbrook. The end of Raman's partnership with Smith came when his partner missed a full toss and was bowled for 98. 'I remember saying, "Bad luck, Mike." Then I got out in the nineties as well.' Caught behind for 94, Raman was part of a mid-order collapse, with England slipping to 235 for six as thunder and lightning threatened the Oval. A late order recovery took England to 361, sufficient to set up another innings victory.

In Raman's absence Northants had drawn with Sussex and beaten Glamorgan by seven wickets thanks to fine batting by Barrick. Crossing London to Lord's, Raman took his recovered form into the match with Middlesex, where he celebrated selection to tour the West Indies with 62 in a century opening stand with Norman. After getting the better of a draw, it was back to the Oval for the final match of the season and a welcome victory by four wickets against a Surrey side with a full-strength attack but deprived early in their first innings of the batting of John Edrich with a broken finger. Surrey, having already surrendered their title to Yorkshire, thereby saw all hopes of finishing as runners up evaporate.

So ended a summer of high hopes but meagre success. Eleventh place in the Championship was Northants' lowest for eight years, but Raman could point to many matches in which victory had just eluded his side in the very closest of finishes. His philosophy had been to throw down the gauntlet whenever he could and to accept opposing captains' challenges. Had three of the very closest games tilted his way, as well they might, Northants would have retained their 1958 position. But at too many crucial moments the final roll of the dice had been against him, fortifying the rather cruel belief that he had not quite the magic touch of his predecessor in judging his declarations. Raman's own batting, especially in the early part of the season, had taken him high up the national averages and he had won a second Test cap, but as he bade farewell to Brookes, still the side's second best batsman, and Tribe, first in the country to complete the double, he will have known that there was little on which to base hopes of short-term glory.

Northamptonshire 1959
back: JS Manning, JG Williamson, A Lightfoot, PA Shenton,
MEJC Norman, AP Arnold, MHJ Allen
front: FH Tyson, GE Tribe, R Subba Row, DW Barrick, KV Andrew

10

'It's about time you had a full toss down the leg side'

The West Indies – and a first Test century

If the MCC team had travelled to Australia in some luxury, the party that departed for the West Indies on 8 December 1959 enjoyed conspicuously fewer comforts. The *TSS Camito*, in which they sailed from Avonmouth, had been built as recently as 1956, but its primary purpose was as a Fyffe's Line banana boat. Whereas a cargo of 1,750 tons of bananas gave the ship some stability on journeys to England, when returning to the West Indies with a lighter load of manufactured goods, the vessel was more at the mercy of the seas. Its provision for only 75 passenger cabins contrasted with the *SS Iberia*'s capacity of over 1,400 passengers, more than half travelling first-class. Whilst all the *Camito* cabins were nominally first-class, there was no air conditioning. Mike Smith, with whom Raman shared a room on the trip, recalls that it was regarded as useful for team bonding to spend ten days together at sea, though he regarded it as a foolish decision to sail in such discomfort: 'The idea that it gave you a chance to get to know one another was always a farce. If anything, it gave you a chance to fall out with each other.'

The disasters of the Australian tour meant that of those with whom Raman had toured only six also made the trip to the West Indies. Peter May and Colin Cowdrey were once again captain and vice-captain, Fred Trueman and Brian Statham were retained to spearhead the pace attack, Roy Swetman, no longer deputy to Godfrey Evans, remained as a wicket-keeper. The sixth man from the earlier tour was Ted Dexter, then a late addition, now one of the last two picks together with pace bowler Alan Moss. Newcomers included Geoff Pullar, Ken Barrington and Mike Smith as batsmen against whom Raman would compete for a place in the Tests. Three spinners were making their first overseas tour: Ray Illingworth and David Allen as off spinners and leg-break bowler Tommy Greenhough. The other wicket-keeper was Raman's Northants colleague Keith Andrew.

Stamping his presence on proceedings as manager was Walter Robins. 'He belonged to a different age.' Raman recalls. 'People who held that position in those were of a different nature. Nothing wrong with them, but they knew their own minds in a way you wouldn't quite find today.' With good reason after the disappointments in Australia, Robins was a man for whom the mantra was 'brighter cricket'. 'A man who puts enjoyment before cost

MCC in the West Indies, 1959/60

RWV Robins (manager), KF Barrington, T Greenhough, G Pullar, AE Moss,
R Illingworth, DA Allen, KV Andrew, R Swetman, H Dalton (masseur)
ER Dexter, FS Trueman, MC Cowdrey, PBH May, JB Statham, MJK Smith, R Subba Row

and enterprise before caution' suggested John Woodcock in *The Times*. In
Raman's eyes Robins' foibles were excused as he had a good sense of humour,
but before the tour was out he would have fallen out with his acting captain
over his safety first tactics.

From the high seas came the first news that would shape Raman's tour.
Where he was pencilled in by some scribes to partner Pullar as an opening
batsman, breakfast reading for those at home on 11 December was that the
tour committee had decided that Cowdrey should open. After docking at
Barbados, the team flew to Grenada, where a matting wicket was provided, the
only one on which they would be asked to play on the tour, for what turned
out to be a low-scoring match. MCC, despite scoring a meagre 121 in their
first innings, still required only 38 for a ten-wicket victory, Greenhough's
leg breaks and googlies having proved far too much for the local batsmen.
Raman, 'relying mainly on deflections' made 21, second highest scorer after
May. Back in Barbados, a drawn two-day match against Barbados Colts saw
Raman reach an unspectacular 28. 'Nudging and deflecting are unlikely to
pay dividends here,' *The Times* correspondent opined.

It was time for the tour to start in earnest. For the four-day match against
Barbados that preceded the first Test on the same Bridgetown ground, Raman

was one of those not selected as MCC fielded what they had hoped might be their Test side. Acknowledged as the strongest of the island teams, the home side rattled up 533 for five with a young Seymour Nurse making 213 and Garry Sobers 154. Then a hitherto unknown Charlie Griffith discomfited the early batsmen, forcing MCC to follow on 295 behind. A more spirited approach almost saved the game, but with Barbados required to make 58 in 25 minutes, Cammie Smith saw them home with three minutes to spare as MCC played on through steady rain.

MCC's sporting spirit in staying on the pitch to the end had won the hearts of the locals, but it came at a price, Statham slipping on the wet ground and damaging a hamstring that was to rule him out of the Test. Paradoxically this injury brought Raman into the reckoning for a place in the Test side. Greenhough, unable to grip the ball in the heat, had not made a case for selection, leaving the selectors with the option of giving a first cap to Allen or packing the batting to ensure a draw by opting for Raman.

Allen won the vote and took his place in an England side for what was destined to be one of the most tedious drawn matches in Test history. England began well, Barrington and Dexter both scoring centuries in their first innings 482. West Indies then began uncertainly. By the end of the third day of a match scheduled for six five-hour days the score was 114 for three. This was a Friday evening. The next wicket fell in the morning session on Tuesday. There had been a rest day, each side of which was a day on which England failed to take a wicket. Yet, so far from taking heavy toll of the tourists' attack, two of the world's most renowned stroke makers, Frank Worrell and Garry Sobers, ground out their runs as they added 399, still a record partnership for West Indies for any wicket against England. The benign nature of the pitch was evident, while Worrell, it seemed, had become so weary that he was barely able to strike the ball off the square. Gerry Alexander, the West Indies captain, eventually showed mercy and declared with Worrell undefeated on 197.

The team moved on to Trinidad, where two matches were to be played before the second Test. Raman now came back into action. Opening with Pullar on the Queen's Park Oval at Port-of-Spain, he top scored in both innings of a match that saw MCC only narrowly avoid the follow-on before going to an exciting win by six wickets. Replying to a Trinidad score of 301 for nine declared, MCC's 171 for nine would have been an even feebler response had Raman not battled for almost three hours in making 49. When Trinidad declared their second innings, MCC were required to get 262 in three and a half hours. They rose to the challenge, Raman and Pullar putting on 44 in 27 minutes with Raman going on to make 73. So far from relying on deflections for his runs, he was now 'fetching the spinners from outside off stump and depositing them in the square leg area.' With all the batsmen contributing, Smith and Dexter added 106 in 67 minutes to take MCC home with ten minutes to spare.

MCC's first innings disarray had come about at the hands of a little known left-arm spinner Charran Singh, playing in only his second first-class match. His five for 57 included four of MCC's top six batsmen, and he might have caused more trouble in the second innings had a catch offered by Raman as soon as he came on been accepted. Curiously omitted from the second of the island matches, he was a bowler of whom the England batsmen would see more in the Test. MCC's second match against Trinidad took first-class cricket for the first time to Guaracara Park at Pointe-a-Pierre on the west coast of the island. The tourists won by ten wickets, stamping their authority from the outset with an opening stand of 174 by Pullar and Cowdrey. Raman, at number three, after sitting with his pads on for over two hours, was out for a single.

For the next Test there was speculation that Raman might replace Illingworth, who had gone wicketless at Bridgetown and was also struggling with the bat. However, England's only change was Statham, fit again, for Moss. From 57 for three on what had looked a good batting pitch, England recovered well and, with centuries from Barrington and Smith, secured a first innings total of 382. Trueman, with five for 35 and Statham, three for 42, then skittled West Indies for 112. But not before trouble had erupted in the stands. At 94 for seven the Test debutant Charran Singh, the local hero after his five wickets in the earlier match, joined his fellow Trinidadian Sonny Ramadhin at the wicket. A record crowd that had assembled in expectation of seeing West Indies batsmen in command were already venting their frustration, and the rum was flowing. The West Indian decline had started with Conrad Hunte given out to a catch in Statham's leg trap. Three batsmen were then adjudged lbw, all by umpire Lee Kow, and there had been a run out. Most of the dismissals had required an umpire's decision and all had been made by a local man from Trinidad.

Now Ramadhin called Singh for an impossibly tight single. Singh could not beat Dexter's throw and once again Lee Kow's finger was raised for what all were agreed was a straightforward decision. It did not stop bottles flying over the protective fence, which soon proved inadequate to prevent a stampede onto the pitch as players and umpires, initially huddled in the middle, ran for the safety of the pavilion. Fortunately the next day was a Sunday, the scheduled rest day for the Test. It allowed time for the Governor and other officials to step in. Talk of abandoning the tour gave way to appeals for civilised behaviour as security was stepped up, and it was agreed that the time that had been lost should be made up. When the match resumed, May chose not to enforce the follow-on. England batted again until they were able to give West Indies ten hours in which to make 501, a score that has still to be reached to win a Test match. Victory came by 256 runs with an hour and 50 minutes to spare.

And so to Jamaica. This was a special moment for Raman for he was to be re-united with his fiancée. He and Anne had announced their engagement shortly before the start of the tour, and Anne now flew out to Jamaica with Ted Dexter's wife Sue, where they watched the third Test match. Demonstrating the friendships that developed between members of opposing sides in those days, Raman's great friend Frank Worrell, whom he had known since their time together on the Commonwealth tour of India, arranged for Raman and Anne to have the use of a brand new car for three weeks during their time in Jamaica. Among cherished

Raman and Anne, newly engaged

memories of the island is a visit to the home of Noel Coward overlooking Montego Bay. There was further hospitality from John Goddard, who had captained two West Indies teams to England, when he invited Anne to extend her stay by joining his family in Barbados, where she enjoyed a blissful holiday.

On the field there was a two-day game against Jamaica Colts, after which came a high-scoring match against a full Jamaica side that included Vincent Lumsden, with whom Raman had played for Cambridge. With 104 from Easton McMorris and 75 from Worrell, the home team made the most of an easy pitch. But their score of 374 was dwarfed by MCC, for whom May at last struck form with 124 and Smith also made a century. Raman, who opened with Cowdrey, contributed 92 to a score of 523 for six with reports that he was 'timing the ball with a certainty he has seldom known out here.' Despite early wickets for Trueman and Worrell nursing a cricked neck and damaged ankle, there was not quite enough time for MCC to force a win, but it left the team in good heart for the ensuing Test.

Relaxing at the Half Moon Bay Hotel, Montego Bay
clockwise from left end of table: Mrs Rostron, Frank Rostron, Ian Peebles, Ron Roberts,
EW Swanton, Mrs Swanton, member of hotel staff, Rex Alston (hidden), Mrs Alston,
Gerry Gomez, John Goddard, Anne, Raman, John Woodcock

Worrell's ankle kept him out of the side and other changes to the West Indies team meant that they entered the match with several of their batsmen short of match practice, while the England side was unchanged. One change that was made was the ending of West Indies' practice of always appointing Test umpires from the host island, Lee Kow bravely flying in from Trinidad. He and his fellow umpire Perry Burke now earned rebukes from reporters for their failure to impose any controls on the short bowling of Wes Hall and Chester Watson, but their bombardment of the England batsmen drew from Cowdrey one of the most courageous innings of his career. A five-hour day yielded just 165 runs for six wickets with Cowdrey 75 not out. His century came the next day as England closed on 277.

West Indies began the fourth day on 291 for two, Sobers unbeaten with 142. When he fell lbw to Trueman having added only five more, the West Indian batsmen went into their shells. As runs dried up, wickets fell, and the lead was contained to 76. By the close Pullar and Cowdrey had almost wiped it out. Next day their stand was extended to 177. But in a match of dramatic twists both batsmen were out at the same score, Cowdrey missing a second hundred by seven runs, after which only May of the remaining batsmen offered much resistance. On the final day England had one wicket intact. Allen and Statham batted for 45 minutes while adding 25. Their modest stand had transformed the time to runs equation. Now needing 230 in 245 minutes, West Indies ended on 175 for six, their chance of victory taking its first blow when Dexter ran out Sobers as he answered a false call from Rohan Kanhai. Then, in the final stages, Kanhai developed cramp and was controversially (and incorrectly) denied a runner by May. Once he became Trueman's fourth victim, all of them bowled, England had made the game safe.

Now came an interlude for the players that typified the relaxed pace of touring before the era of crowded schedules and multiple formats of the game. Arriving in Antigua to play the Leeward Islands, the team found among the spectators Sir Anthony Eden, the former prime minister, who was making use of his sunshine home on the island to complete the writing of his memoirs. With Trueman and Statham resting between Test matches and enjoying time on Sir Anthony's private beach, MCC fielded a weakened attack. The regular Test spinners were given few overs as the leg breaks of Greenhough and Barrington took the lion's share of the bowling, while one other spinner also turned an arm, Raman ending with figures of 16 – 4 – 50 – 2. Back in his principal role he then scored 110 as he and Cowdrey, who made 115, replied to the islanders' 296 with an opening stand of 210. On a docile pitch at the Recreation Ground in St John's, where Brian Lara would many years later twice record Test cricket's highest score, runs were there for the picking. There was another hundred from Dexter and 86 from Barrington, but the pitch ended the winner as the Islands lost only three wickets in their second innings.

Peter May, whose wife was another to have flown out to the sunshine, had taken time off from the match in Antigua, but he was back to captain the side in the next match at Georgetown in what was then British Guiana (now Guyana). There was a lack lustre first day as the home batsmen made 184 for two. Next day Basil Butcher proceeded to a hundred and Clyde Walcott, who had not featured in the Tests, injected some life into the innings, which closed after nine hours at 375 for six. Raman bowled two overs just before the close. Next day he had an extended spell. 'From MCC's point of view,' wrote John Woodcock, 'there was more than a passing interest in the bowling of Subba Row.' Raman had forsaken his once traditional leg breaks in favour of off spin and had helped to tie the batsmen down with a steady line outside off stump, giving rise to speculation that his bowling might earn him a place in the Test team ahead of Illingworth or Allen.

Such speculation was soon to prove academic. The match petered out in a predictable draw after Pullar and Cowdrey had opened with a stand of 281. Raman made only 16, but of greater concern to the team was the absence of May. He had not fielded on the second day and was unable to bat. It was now revealed that there was a recurrence of the abdominal problems he had suffered during the English summer. Those close to the captain had long felt that he was not fully fit and that this had affected his form with the bat. The problem was to prove more serious than at first feared, but the short-term news was that Cowdrey would lead the side in the fourth Test with Raman taking May's place in the batting line-up.

With a delayed start England, having won the toss, made 152 for two on the first day with Cowdrey on 65. Raman had come in at the fall of the first wicket and had immediately injected some urgency into the running between the wickets. He was looking confident when, on 27, he had the misfortune to be dismissed by the worst ball of the day – a Sobers long hop that he had tried to paddle to fine leg but only succeeded in steering into Alexander's grateful hands behind the wicket. The middle and lower order batting, with the exception of Allen, offered little resistance and England were all out for 295.

A few showers and the slowness of the early West Indian batsmen meant that even with 145 from Sobers at number four, Alexander's declaration at 402 for eight left all too little time to bowl England out a second time. Despite the speculation before the match Raman had not bowled in the innings, but he had a vital role to play when he came to the wicket at the start of the final day. Overnight England had lost two wickets, Pullar to the last ball of the day, and when Raman and Dexter resumed they led by three runs. Dexter had batted ahead of Raman, who had chipped a bone in his left hand during the first innings and was now heavily bandaged. It was to prove a day in which the tension gradually eased. The two Cambridge Blues added 148, both making centuries, but had wickets fallen early in the day it could have been a different outcome for England, especially as Barrington was nursing a bruised elbow. By the time Raman's hundred was approaching, the game was long dead. His friend Frank Worrell came up to him. 'He told me, "It's about time you had a full toss down the leg side." I couldn't believe my ears, but Frank was not the sort of chap who would con me, and there it was. Bang!' Then I was out next ball, lbw Worrell.'

John Woodcock's admiration for Raman owed little to any aesthetic qualities in his batting. Marking his first Test century, he now wrote: 'Subba Row is one of the great stickers in English cricket, however unconvincing he may sometimes appear.' He later contrasted Dexter, 'a player of the highest class' with his more utilitarian partner: 'Subba Row kept nudging and cutting and pushing and scotching, his shoulders hunched, his stance open, his stride between wickets long and loping.'

As the match ended came news that May's tour was over. He flew back to England as did Statham whose young son was dangerously ill. Raman was appointed vice-captain of the depleted side. With Cowdrey taking a rest, it was Raman who led MCC onto the field for their three-day match against Berbice, an inland region within British Guiana. On a featherbed pitch two Guyanese Test cricketers enjoyed an unbroken stand of 290, Joe Solomon making a double century and Basil Butcher 131. There were three century makers for MCC, the most notable 183 by Jim Parks, who had been drafted into the party from a coaching assignment in the Caribbean. This innings ensured that he would replace Swetman, who had endured wretched form with the bat, for the final Test, which entailed the tourists returning to the scene of their earlier triumph at the Queen's Park Oval in Trinidad.

The objective now was to deny West Indies any chance of winning and thereby consummate a series win that would have seemed a mirage when the tour had begun in Barbados. There was another Cowdrey century in England's 393, to which Raman's contribution was 22. Then West Indies declared 55 behind, capturing Cowdrey's wicket before the close of the fourth day. The low point for England came at 148 for six. They were only 203 ahead with the top batting and night-watchman Allen all dismissed, Raman among them for only 13. Parks then joined Smith. They stayed together until the close, which came at 238 for six, with the more aggressive Parks on 55.

Next day, the last of the tour, the drama was in the dressing room. On the pitch Parks and Smith were engrossed in putting the game beyond West Indies' reach, eventually adding a record 197 for the seventh wicket; but away from the action the captain was being berated by his manager to declare and see if he could wrap up the series with a second win. 'Make a game of it,' he urged. What we have we hold was the strong consensus of the team, brought forcibly home to Walter Robins by the acting senior professional Fred Trueman. 'You ain't no business in here. Get out!' he is alleged to have told the manager.

Determined that no opportunity to fly the flag for cricket should be missed, MCC had decreed that this should not be the end of the tour. Before the team flew home, they visited British Honduras, now Belize, where two one-day games were played. In front of crowds of over 4,000 Raman led the tourists in both matches. Making sure that all his players should have a bat and most bowl a few overs, he presided over two comfortable wins for the tourists. There was a fifty for Raman in the second match, in which he had opened with Walter Robins, and with wickets so cheap that Swetman was able to take three in the first match and Pullar three in the second, it was Raman whose spinners wrapped up the tail in the second match, allowing him to sign off with four for 26.

11

'A workman in the Birthday Honours'

A regular England place

Cricket was to take second place in Raman's priorities as he returned from the West Indies. On Thursday 21 April 1960 he and Anne were married at the Queen's Chapel of the Savoy in London. Anne's brother-in-law, the Reverend Peter Gotelee, conducted the service assisted by the Reverend Cyril Cresswell, the Queen's chaplain. Raman's brother Stanley was best man. The wedding was followed by a reception at 55 Park Lane, with attendance swollen by many friends who had been at one of the lunches of the British Sportsmen's Club regularly held at the Savoy.

Raman and Anne Harrison had first met, they delight in relating, on a blind date back in 1954. Anne had been planning an outing to the cinema, when the friend with whom she was going received a telephone call. 'It was from her boyfriend,' Anne now relates. 'He said, "What are you doing this evening? Can we go out?" She said, "Sorry, I'm going out with Anne, but if you've got a friend who'd like to come, we'll go out as a foursome."' 'That was the downfall of me,' Raman interjects. 'The boyfriend was Graham Bond, with whom I played bad rugby.' Raman completed the party to the cinema and he was soon testing Anne's interest in sport by inviting her to watch him play fives and squash in a match for the Jesters.

Raman and Anne had announced their engagement in November 1959 shortly before Raman's departure to the West Indies, and as Anne waved the MCC party off, she knew that they would soon be reunited on the tour. Back in England, she continued to work in the advertising industry, where she was employed by Mather & Crowther, a leading agency of the day, later to become Ogilvy & Mather and finally morph into Ogilvy's, retaining the name of one of the legendary figures of the business. She recalls working for Ernest Lough whose name will for ever be associated with his chorister's rendering of 'O for the Wings of a Dove' from Mendelssohn's 'Hear my Prayer', which became EMI's first classical record to sell over a million copies.

Anne continued to live with her parents in Croydon, while the young couple awaited the completion of their first house, where they would live for five years before moving to their present home close by. Meanwhile, in Northamptonshire Raman was now lodging in a rectory in Weston Flavell, then a village on the outskirts of the town but now more heavily built up,

Wedding Day

where Anne was able to visit at weekends. Illustrating her talent for retaining friendships, she and Raman for many years remained in touch with Douglas Hopkins, the incumbent, and his wife Marie.

Marriage was only one factor in Raman's deliberations about the shape of his life and how long he could afford to stay in the first-class game. He had always been an amateur at a time when it was virtually unheard of for a man of his background and education to forsake that status. Illustrating what was involved if an amateur decided to turn professional, Paul Gibb, a pre-war Cambridge Blue, had played for Yorkshire as an amateur, but his switch to the professional ranks with Essex and subsequent career as an umpire cost him his MCC membership. His final employment, as a bus driver with his identity unknown to colleagues, rather emphasised the social consequences of his career pattern. More recently, when Brian Parsons, a Cambridge Blue and former pupil of Brighton College, had signed as a professional for Surrey in 1958, it was a striking exception to normal patterns of behaviour. For Raman there was never any question of playing other than as an amateur, but he still needed to earn a living. In this he was no different from most other amateurs playing full-time first-class cricket: they could be paid legitimate, and sometimes generous, expenses, but from somewhere they needed a proper income.

A few players were fortunate to have an employer who, if not wholly philanthropic, could see value in having on the payroll someone whose status as a sports star might be of some benefit to the company. Peter May and John Warr, for instance, had jobs in the City, while Doug Insole worked for Wimpey. Then there were those who were employed by their counties in an office role. Some such as Charles Palmer, Wilfred Wooller and Desmond Eagar fully merited the salaries they earned, but more questions could be asked of others such as Mike Smith at Warwickshire or Donald Carr at Derbyshire, whose counties had exceptionally able secretaries, well capable of running affairs with minimal assistance and not, perhaps, making great demands of their county captains who were employed as paid assistants. And what of Trevor Bailey? He may have been in evidence shifting score boxes and the like before the start of play in county matches, but how did this square with spending whole winters abroad?

It was all of concern to the powers that be at MCC, but those required to look into amateur status faced an almost insoluble dilemma. A Special Committee on Amateur Status, chaired by the Duke of Norfolk, was dominated by those who wished to preserve the amateur in first-class cricket for the supposed special values he brought to the game – and his contribution on the social side, some stressed; but they wanted him to be a 'proper' amateur. Yet, tacitly or otherwise, they recognized that long past were the days when shoals of young men had the private means to be unconcerned about earning a supplementary income. If there was ever a circle that could not be squared, this surely was it.

Selected professionals, invited to give their views to the wholly amateur committee, said that no grudges were harboured against the man who received only expenses, but resentment could arise where an amateur was seen to be earning more than the professionals alongside whom he played without any appearance of doing much work around the office. There were also anomalies on tour, which had triggered the enquiry in the first place. Professionals had complained of the liberal expenses allowed to the amateurs, while those same amateurs were in turn protesting that they could barely afford to tour. Here the committee's proposal was that 'broken time' payment, compensation for loss of earnings, should be available to amateurs, but their expenses and those of professionals should be the same. Yet emphasising the humbug of the whole arrangement, it was felt that the compensation paid should be related not to any salary the amateur might be earning elsewhere but to the amount paid as a tour fee to the professionals. There was even a suggestion that a married man's broken time payment should be higher than that of a bachelor.

Bubbling beneath the surface was another uncomfortable truth: the top order batting in England teams of the day was heavily dependent on amateurs. Of the batsmen taken to the West Indies, for instance, only two, Pullar and Barrington, were professionals, while five – May, Cowdrey, Smith, Dexter and Subba Row – were amateurs. Such talent had to be kept within the game for as long as possible, all were agreed, especially as the Oxbridge pipeline was continuing to deliver more Blues who would soon be challenging for Test places, Bob Barber, Tony Lewis and Roger Prideaux among them.

The complex mesh of committees that were set up and referred issues to each other has been lucidly described by Charles Williams in his *Gentlemen & Players*. Laced with wit and an understandable sarcasm, Williams' book exposes some of the work undertaken by a separate Amateur Status Standing Committee, whose remit was to identify individuals whose remuneration offended the accepted if rather vague code. Testing the patience of many of the counties and branded by Wilfred Wooller as 'The Star Chamber', the committee arranged for questionnaires to be circulated to assist in their enquiries. Counties were asked to name a) the registered amateurs whom they employed directly, giving details of the duties carried out, and b) those who received financial assistance from any body associated with the County Club.

With the first category a need was found to ask further questions about the secretarial duties carried out by Carr at Derbyshire and by Peter Richardson for Worcestershire. Names of special interest in the second category were Raman and Reg Simpson at Notts, while Wooller's wrath was kindled by the committee daring to probe the employment details of his planned successor as captain of Glamorgan, Ossie Wheatley. 'Mind your own business' was the tone of several responses, but the committee was satisfied by the amount of work done by Carr, while Richardson's position at Worcestershire became academic once he had decided to qualify for Kent and turn professional. An acceptable arrangement was cobbled together for Wheatley at Glamorgan and Notts reported that Simpson's contract had ended. This meant, in hunting terms, that whilst other quarry had slipped the net, Raman was the prize capture.

Raman had by now taken a job working on the publicity side for the Noel Gay Organisation, music publishers in London, and Northamptonshire had struck an agreement whereby he was to be paid £1,000 a year for a period of five years 'to cover compensation for loss of earnings, accommodation expenses while living in Northampton, travelling expenses, hotels and meals, up-keep of clothing and equipment, Captain's allowance for entertainment and tips.' Within this sum £450 was regarded as compensation for loss of earnings; but in MCC's eyes such payments were only permissible for winter tours, not for playing during the English summer. Raman had been a marked target earlier in the saga with the unacceptable nature of his contract notified to Northants as early as the autumn of 1958, though when the cudgels were taken up by Ken Turner a moratorium was agreed until April 1960, during which time the various committees at MCC continued to convene and chew over the same issues.

Somehow Raman survived to play the 1960 season, with Turner obliged to write that 'Mr Subba Row has told my Committee that, although he hopes to struggle through the season, he cannot hope to do so in future years and has intimated that it must be considered that he will not be able to continue to play after 1960.' The next year Turner would be embroiled in further correspondence, but his 1960 letter went on to say: 'The loss of this Test cricketer to the game is a prospect which my Committee view with dismay, and they have instructed me to inform you of Mr Subba Row's intentions.' Paradoxically it would all end shortly after Raman had retired with some of those who had fought hardest to keep the amateur, notably the Duke of Norfolk, realising that they had been attempting mission impossible. By the start of the 1963 season the cherished distinction would have been buried for good with all county players henceforth regarded as 'cricketers'.

Northants were to see little of their amateur captain in 1960. The severity of Peter May's illness in the West Indies may not have been fully understood when he had to fly back from the Caribbean, but it was to keep him out of cricket for the whole of the English summer. A place thereby opened up in

Gentlemen At Ease, 1960
AC Smith, AJ Corran, RM Prideaux, DM Sayer, AM Hurd
RW Barber, DB Carr, MC Cowdrey, R Subba Row, MJK Smith
ER Dexter

the England team and Raman was chosen for the series, missing only the last of the five Tests after breaking his thumb in the fourth. It was an injury that ended his season only three weeks into July.

There were to be only ten championship matches in the season for Raman, seven of them ahead of the first Test against South Africa. These seven matches yielded three losses and four draws. So, when their captain departed for the Test, only Leicestershire lay beneath Northants in the table. Raman had nevertheless given the tourists evidence of his personal good form with 108 at Northampton, as the South Africans suffered the first defeat of their trip, Northants winning by four wickets in the final over. It was, perhaps, a Pyrrhic victory, coming after the visitors had twice declared. Indeed, after they had scored 461 for 3 in their first innings, it was only Raman's stubborn batting that averted the follow-on. Fortunate to win Northants may have been, but Mick Norman, who played an important part with the bat, remembers that the visitors rewarded their first conquerors with a case of South African wine.

Other good early season innings for Raman included a century against Surrey and nineties against Yorkshire and Warwickshire, all of them away from Northampton. His fluent unbeaten 147 at the Oval had echoes of the record-breaking stand two years earlier as Albert Lightfoot also reached three figures, helping his captain add 214 and secure first innings points.

The county's disappointing start to the season above all reflected the loss of Tribe. In his absence it was disheartening that the early season form of Manning, who had taken 110 championship wickets the previous year, was so poor that by the end of May he had played his last game for Northants. This did, however, pave the way for the return of Allen, who became the leading wicket-taker. But it was only after new faces were introduced that the team's fortunes improved – though Raman was all too seldom there to share in the revival.

The first of the newcomers appeared against Derbyshire in the last match before Raman's departure. David Larter was an exceptionally tall pace bowler, who had joined from Suffolk. A quiet and gentle giant in the dressing room, he quickly made an impact on the pitch, providing Tyson with the opening partner he had always needed, while Brian Crump, whose debut came a week later, was soon to prove his worth as an all-rounder. Larter headed the county's bowling averages for the season, while Crump finished second to Raman in the batting as well as taking 41 championship wickets with his off spinners.

Raman first played with Crump in the county team when they combined to add 198 against Cambridge University. The next time they were together was against Yorkshire at Northampton, where Raman re-joined the team immediately after playing in the second Test. When Crump joined his captain on the last day, the score was 118 for four. A target of 286 meant that 168 had still to be scored, and just an hour and three quarters remained in which to do it. Most counties would have settled for a draw, and this was the limit of Raman's ambition when the partnership began, but Raman was in prime form and, as so often when he was in good touch, the runs were accumulating without any memorable shots.

Brian Crump takes up the story. Though undefeated in the end, he believes himself to have been out twice. 'Fred Trueman was fielding at short leg. I played it towards him. He caught it and I started to walk off. But the umpire said "Not out", so I stayed in. Fred made hardly any comment – he just accepted it. I carried on, then I got run out. I was running towards the pavilion, and when they threw the ball in, I knew I was out. So I just ran through the crease towards the pavilion. All of a sudden the umpire's waving. "Not out. Come back!" He said he couldn't see the chap who'd broken the wicket. So back again!'

On they went, the runs still accumulating. 'We can win this,' Brian remembers his captain telling him. With 23 needed from three overs 13 were taken off Fred Trueman, and when the world's best fast bowler, in his own estimation, began the final over, Northants still required three to win. Trueman resorted to bouncers, which Crump ducked. After four balls Raman spoke to his young partner. 'You've got to take him on,' he said. The next ball went to the midwicket boundary. It was Northants' first win of the season. It had come against the reigning champions, who were at the head of the table again. Raman, who had led the assault, had made 135 in 158 minutes. 'One of the highlights of my career,' his partner remembers. 'There was hell to play with the Yorkshire lads because they'd lost the game. Fred was brilliant. He came up and shook my hand and said, "Well done, lad." But Closey was absolutely livid, moaning about the skipper.'

There was another win for Northants in the next match, Worcestershire succumbing by five wickets, after Larter had taken six for 26 in the first innings, before Raman was reclaimed by Test cricket. In his absence Northants' revival continued. After rain washed out the match against Leicestershire, there was a 72-run win at Gloucester. Raman was back for the next fixture at Bath, where he ended 48 not out as his cool head steered his county home by six wickets after taking up a sporting challenge from Somerset captain Harold Stephenson to score 174 in 145 minutes. Northants were now tenth in the table, and their captain had played a key role in their recovery. The improved form continued for a while under Barrick's captaincy. At one point Northants stood sixth, but with both Barrick and Raman absent over the closing weeks the wins dried up and the county had to settle for ninth, only two places above the previous year but higher than had seemed likely at the end of June.

Raman's average of over 57 from his ten matches dwarfed his colleagues in this transitional season, where hopes for the future founded on Larter and Crump were balanced by a disappointing return from young Jim Watts and rather expensive wickets from his leg-spinning brother Peter. Reynolds had recovered from his injury and returned to forge an opening partnership with Norman, allowing Raman, when playing, to bat in the middle order. In Raman's absence Donald Ramsamooj, an aggressive batsman from Trinidad, had come into the side late in the season. But there were farewells to Frank Tyson and to Peter Arnold, who had dropped out of the side in mid-season. In 1961 there would be another year of rebuilding. It would not be easy.

However mixed Raman's fortunes with Northants, he could look back on a season in which he travelled from marginal Test candidate to holding down a well-merited place in the England side. His early season form was rewarded by inclusion in the twelve chosen for the first Test at Edgbaston. Raman's name was nevertheless among those who, it was speculated, might be missing from the final eleven. In the end a run of wretched scores in county cricket meant that Barrington was omitted and first caps were awarded to

Bob Barber, one of five county captains in the team, and Glamorgan's Peter Walker. There was further debate about where Raman might bat, Cowdrey having prospered as an opener in the West Indies though always preferring a place in the middle order. In the event Cowdrey opened and Raman went in at number four after Dexter.

For the visitors it was never the happiest of tours. They had been greeted by anti-apartheid protestors on arrival, some waving placards with the challenging words 'What about Subba Row?' Well what about him? By early April he had already been named to captain A.E.R. Gilligan's XI in an end of season festival match at Hastings, when it was reported that the West Indians Sobers and Kanhai would also be playing. The South Africans had been instructed not to talk about politics, but their professed willingness to play against cricketers of any race was perhaps being tacitly tested by this early announcement.

The tour was also one in which the South African team was outgunned throughout the Test series, having little answer to England's pace attack, while further indignity was to come in the second Test at Lord's with the no balling of pace bowler Geoff Griffin. At least they began on a more positive note. Cowdrey won the toss. After pondering long on the matter, he decided to bat in blustery conditions with rain a constant threat – and he was soon caught behind the wicket off Neil Adcock for only 3. Opening partner Pullar made batting look like hard labour as Dexter revealed the best of his strokes. Raman, coming to the wicket at 80 on Pullar's departure, also batted in pedestrian mode that suffered by comparison with Dexter's fluent driving off the back foot. On Dexter's dismissal at 100, Raman was joined by Smith. They took the score to 175 by the close, Raman on 32. Next day he progressed to 56, England's top scorer with an innings in which 'he endured all but four hours without discovering his timing.'

England's 292 was to prove beyond a South African side beset by a weak batting line-up, the three principal bowlers, Statham, Trueman and Illingworth sharing the wickets. When England batted again with a lead of 106, Cowdrey was accompanied by Raman, Pullar having broken a bone in his hand on the first day. The captain failed again but Raman's 32 was bettered only by Walker at number eight. England duly won by 100 runs with the wickets again shared.

Pullar's injury meant that Raman was no longer an understudy opener for the Lord's Test. Again Cowdrey won the toss and chose to bat in conditions which offered the fast bowers some help, and again he failed with the bat. At the end of a much interrupted day Raman was still securing an end. Undefeated on 36 in a score of 114 for two, his batting had once more suffered from

Raman batting against South Africa
The wicket-keeper is John Waite

comparison with the elegance of Dexter. The dividend came on the resumption as Raman soldiered on to 90 with only five fours, allowing John Woodcock to describe him as 'a workman who seldom catches the eye but finishes up, as it were, in the Birthday Honours.' With 99 from Smith and eleven wickets for Statham, England were soon on the way to an innings victory, but not without unpleasantness already hovering over the legitimacy of Griffin's bowling action.

Having been no balled eleven times by umpire Frank Lee, Griffin had escaped the less forgiving eye of Syd Buller until an exhibition match that took place in the afternoon to provide some cricket for the Monday crowd to watch. Making clear that he saw every delivery as unfair, Buller ensured that Griffin, who had earlier had special remedial coaching at Alf Gover's school, would play no more international cricket. That the entertainment provided coincided with the visit of the Queen compounded the sadness for all involved – not least for Buller, who had done his duty as he saw it, and for Griffin, who remained with the touring party without bowling again, his Test career over at the age of 21. He played seven more matches for Rhodesia, none of them in the Currie Cup. When his action failed to satisfy a local umpire, he accepted that he had reached the end of the road.

The third Test at Tent Bridge saw England seal the series, this time thanks primarily to the bowling of Trueman. Raman contributed 30 to an opening stand of 57 with Cowdrey, who at last found his true form, and when supine South African batting meant that only 49 were required for victory, he remained undefeated, England's only alarms coming from the relentless rain that did all it could to rescue a lost cause for South Africa.

Rain, so often associated with Old Trafford, allowed no play in the fourth Test until the third day. When England batted, Pullar, recovered from injury, opened with Raman. Needing to make up time, England were all out for 260 before close of play, Raman having ensured a steady start with 27 in just over two hours before being trapped lbw by Adcock. Roy McLean then hit South Africa's only hundred of the series, but his glorious attacking innings was not enough to secure a lead, and there was too little time left in the match for England to force a victory. After McLean's innings had ended England were briefly detained by a ninth wicket stand involving the former Kent player Sid O'Linn. Having hit Allen for six, O'Linn wafted at Statham and offered a hard chance to Raman in the slips. The catch went to ground but not before it had broken Raman's thumb. He did not bat in the second innings, and it was to be the end of his season. With 55.56 he headed the national first-class averages. For England in the Tests he was deprived of the top spot only by Pullar making 175 to save the final match of the series.

12

'For God'sake, Raman, don't get out!'

Success as an Ashes opener

Raman was now an established member of the England team, but in the winter of 1960/61 no full MCC team went on tour, though Dennis Silk took an A side to New Zealand that included a few of the younger players with whom Raman had played in the summer's Tests as well as recognizing the talent of Larter from Northants. For Raman there was at last a full winter of work with the Noel Gay Organisation. The firm had been founded in 1938 by Reginald Armitage, music composer for shows such as 'Me and My Girl', who used his show business name in forming a company to publish his own songs and light music. In the 1950s, Reginald's son Richard formed Noel Gay Artists to supply singers to sing his father's hits. By the 1960s the company was acting more widely as agent for many household names, not merely musical performers such as singer Paul Jones and pianist Russ Conway but also those from the wider world of entertainment among them David Frost and John Cleese. The company still operates from Denmark Street with a string of clients from all corners of the entertainment world. Raman remembers Russ Conway with particular affection – a man with more than a passing interest in cricket though no playing credentials. At the time Raman knew him he was at the height of his fame with 20 chart hits in the years between 1957 and 1963 before his career was blighted by ill health.

Destined to be Raman's last season in the first-class game, the summer of 1961 was awaited with the special passion and interest only an Ashes series can generate. But before he could savour the challenges that lay ahead Raman found his amateur status once again the focus of attention at Lord's. Northants had been forced to cancel the contract which had brought him a guaranteed £1,000 a year. A pleading letter from Ken Turner cut no ice with MCC. Turner was to be recognized as one of the forward-looking thinkers in the game, but at this stage he was a young pup in establishment eyes. Not for him letters starting 'Dear Ken'; it was 'Dear Turner'. Except for truly formal notifications, when 'Dear Sir' was the prescribed mode of address. And so it was in a letter of 16 February in which the Secretary of MCC reminded him of the conditions laid down in the report of the Special Committee going on to say that 'it is made clear in the Report that broken time payments to amateurs when playing in England shall not be allowed.' Northants minutes reveal that an anonymous gentleman had offered £500 to cover Raman's loss of earnings. Presumably because no contract was involved, everyone was happy. A committee with one or two well-heeled gentlemen could have its benefits.

Raman had unfinished business at Northants, but his principal focus would be on the Test matches, where one batting place in the England team might be threatened by the return to cricket of Peter May. Acknowledging Raman's status in the game, he was chosen to lead MCC in an early season match against Surrey at Lord's. His side included Test stars Garry Sobers and Fazal Mahmood, the Pakistan seam bowler, as well as a number of promising young cricketers of passing interest to the selectors, among them Mick Norman and Brian Crump from Northants. A drawn game, a victim of the weather, provided Raman with the chance to show that he was in decent nick as he shared a stand of 72 with Sobers, who made a dazzling century.

Raman remained at Lord's for his county's first match of the season. Never a bad place to score runs with many of cricket's most discerning aficionados in attendance, Raman dominated the Northants innings with 93 not out in a total of 266 to secure a first innings lead, but a hip damaged in stretching to make a square cut had caused a temporary retirement in mid innings. So it was that, as Northants chased 161 in 125 minutes on the final day, their captain limped to the wicket at number nine to see his side home by three wickets. Prophetic words in the press that, with this victory, his side might be challengers for the County Championship would soon prove to be the stuff of dreams.

They were to beat Derbyshire at Northampton later in the month but would go without another win until the last match of June, when Raman returned from the second Test match. By this time there had been eight championship losses, seven of them in succession, and Northants were at the bottom of the table. Raman's own form had been patchy. After his heroics at Lord's he had had a few useful starts, but when he was chosen for the first Test, he had passed fifty only twice. Along the way he had played as opener for MCC against the Australians only to fall early to Alan Davidson, though he made a spirited 37 in the second innings. The lowest point came before he travelled from Northampton to join the England side at Edgbaston. He departed fresh from scoring 0 and 2 in a 256 run loss to Surrey.

With May having declared himself unfit for selection, England's established top six batsmen all played. When Cowdrey won the toss, he may have had doubts about the wisdom of batting, but he nevertheless decided that Raman and Pullar should set the tone for the series. With rain interrupting the morning and afternoon sessions, England struggled to 180 for eight. Conditions had suited the medium pace of Ken McKay, and only one man had countered the uncertainties of the sawdust-covered pitch –

Raman. His 59 was comfortably England's best score. Though eight others had reached double figures, the best was Barrington with 21. All out for 195 next morning, England were soon witnessing two masterful stroke-makers, Neil Harvey and Norman O'Neill, enjoying a pitch that had rolled out to provide an easy batting surface. 359 for five overnight, Australia proceeded to 516 for nine before inviting England to do their best to save the match.

The England cause had already been helped by the Saturday weather delaying the Australian declaration. Then, when England batted, there was an early close. Raman and Pullar, facing a deficit of 321, escaped to the pavilion after only two overs. More rain on Monday further frustrated the Australians as England reached 106 for one with Raman on 68, having been the dominant partner in a combination of two serial nudgers. There was now a real prospect of escape for England as the pitch no longer offered much to the bowlers. And so it proved. Dexter made a magisterial 180 not out, but it had been the earlier limpet-like batting of Raman that had done at least as much to save the match for England. Eventually bowled for 112, he had joined the select band with a century in his first Ashes match. It was, in the words of *The Times*, 'an achievement as much of temperament as technique.' Four players with Indian blood had taken part in Ashes Tests, Ranjitsinhji, his nephew Duleep, the Nawab of Pataudi and now Raman – and all four had marked their first match with a hundred.

For the second Test at Lord's May returned, though not as captain. Since their defeat at Melbourne England had played 18 Tests without loss. It was a run that was soon to end, though not before another sequence was extended: for the twelfth time in succession England's captain won the toss. As at Edgbaston, it was to prove an uncertain benefit with the pitch more malevolent than expected. Cloud cover assisted swing, while the bounce was unpredictable, especially at the Nursery end, where a mysterious ridge regularly contributed to the batsmen's uncertainty. The left-arm pace bowler Alan Davidson, on his third tour of England, was soon making the most of the conditions and with better support from his fielders, who allowed each of the top three batsmen a life, he might have blown England away sooner. First to go was Pullar at 26. Raman and Dexter then added 61, but both fell at the same score, Raman for 48, England's best, as he missed a long hop in trying to reach his half-century. Wickets thereafter fell steadily and the innings closed on 206, Davidson claiming five for 42. Overnight Australia lost Colin McDonald and Bobby Simpson for 42.

Next day Bill Lawry progressed to 130, taking his side to 286 for eight. Luck had not gone England's way, and on the Saturday the screw was gradually tightened. It began with precious further runs added for the last two wickets

Raman hits out against Australia in the first Test

to put Australia 134 ahead. By the time the lead had been overhauled half the England side were gone, Raman caught behind off Davidson for 8 to start the rot. On the Monday there was high drama as Australia, needing only 69, were 19 for four, with Trueman and Statham bowling like men possessed. But Peter Burge took control and Australia went one up in the series.

At Headingley there was again a pitch that favoured the bowlers, this time the possible cause an inappropriate chemical applied a few weeks before the match. At the toss there were two different captains from the second Test. At Lord's Neil Harvey had deputised for Richie Benaud, who was nursing a damaged shoulder, while for England May now took back the reins from his long-term deputy. After Benaud had at last called correctly, uncertain bounce was the principal problem facing his batsmen. England were without Statham, 40-year-old Les Jackson replacing him to win a second England cap twelve years after his first. Jackson supported Trueman well with two wickets in each innings. But it was the Yorkshireman, with five for 58, who was the principal destroyer on the opening day, the tourists, at one time 187 for two, folding to 237 all out. In reply England began steadily, reaching 54 before Raman was lbw to Davidson for 35. Pullar battled on to 54 and there was 93 from Cowdrey, but with few middle order runs England's lead was only 62. It was soon to seem a decisive advantage as Trueman now excelled himself, ending with six for 30. Only Harvey, whose 73 had been top score in Australia's first innings, showed much resistance, with 53 out of a total of 120. A target of only 59 made victory for England a formality.

The series stood one all moving to Old Trafford and one of the most dramatic of post-war Ashes Tests. But before this match Raman had another encounter with the tourists. His Northamptonshire side may have been languishing in the Championship, but for the match against the Australians they rose to the occasion. The wickets were shared around as the visitors were restricted to 313, with O'Neill, 99 not out at lunch, claiming the lion's share with 142. Norman and Reynolds replied with an opening stand of 128 in which both passed 60, and when Raman declared 24 behind, Lightfoot had reached 80. It was an imaginative declaration. With two players absent, McDonald having injured his wrist in the first innings and wicket-keeper Wally Grout feeling unwell, the remaining batsmen mustered only 173 in Australia's second innings. This set Northants to make 198 in 145 minutes. Norman led the way with 84, Raman weighed in with 33 and Lightfoot again passed fifty. He was at the wicket with Crump as Davidson prepared to bowl the final over with Northants still requiring four runs to win. There was a single to Crump off the second ball, but he was then run out, bringing Malcolm Scott to the wicket. He hit a two to level the scores, swung wildly at the next delivery, then, with one needed from the final ball, attempted a bye only to find Lightfoot failing to respond.

For the fourth Test at Old Trafford an unfit Cowdrey was replaced by Close and Allen came in for Lock. Jackson made way for Statham, but he may have been disappointed to see the third seamer berth go to Jack Flavell of Worcestershire, who had made his case for inclusion when bowling the Players to an emphatic victory over the Gentlemen at Lord's. When Australia batted first, there was immediate success for England, Statham dismissing Simpson in the second over. At 51 came his next success, Raman diving to grasp a chance at second slip just as Harvey was looking dangerous. It was a brilliant effort that caused the batsman to linger a moment at the crease. He looked at Raman, who gave a nod to confirm a clean catch, and Harvey was on his way. 'It's how it was done in those days,' says Raman.

When rain ended play for the day in mid-afternoon, Australia were 124 for four. O'Neill, in continual discomfort ducking and weaving against the fast bowlers, had finally collapsed on his stumps attempting to avoid a Trueman bouncer, and a cavalier stroke by Burge had given Flavell his first Test wicket. The one batsman to look comfortable was Lawry in his first Test series. Next day he was soon out for 74, the tail was blown away and Australia were all out for 190. Raman was caught in the slips off Davidson for 2, and Dexter soon followed, but a stand of 111 between Pullar and May meant that England closed the day three behind the Australian total with only three wickets down. Hopes that the Saturday crowd might see a century from the England captain came to nought as he fell for 95, but 78 from Barrington was the principal contribution in building a lead of 177.

Adding 63 overnight, Australia's openers had begun to redress the balance. Lawry, already missed at slip by Raman, progressed to 102 next day, and the close came at 331 for six, McKay and Davidson the not out batsmen. England's catching had been fallible, with Raman one of the culprits having failed to take another chance offered by McKay. With Australia leading by 154, the pundits agreed that the game was England's if they could get early wickets. On the resumption they came quicker than any had dared hope. In 15 balls Allen removed McKay, Benaud and Grout at no personal cost. Just a month past his twentieth birthday, Graham McKenzie had shown his batting credentials at Lord's. He needed the same obduracy now, but Davidson had made few runs in the series and England waited to apply the coup de grace. Davidson took care to shield his partner from Allen, leading Trueman to suggest to May that a different off spinner should bowl at McKenzie. So Close was given the ball, but his full tosses eased the pressure, McKenzie helping himself to easy runs.

May's next move, as recalled by the bowler, was to suggest that Allen might give the ball more air. Having bowled nine overs for two runs, Allen saw Davidson take 20 from his next six balls with two mighty sixes. The batsman looks back on this moment. 'One gets away with certain things,' he says with a chuckle. 'There was only one way to go. I made up my mind to go after him.' The initiative had now shifted. May was on the defensive, removing Allen from the line of fire; but his quicker bowlers could not achieve the breakthrough. The last wicket stand had reached 98 when Flavell bowled McKenzie for 32. What had promised to be a comfortable quest for victory had turned into a requirement to score 256 in 230 minutes. It was either side's match, but for Australia, as holders of the Ashes, a win was less imperative.

Pullar and Raman began brightly, adding 40 before Pullar was caught for 26. Ted Dexter then entered the fray. Since the first Test he had not enjoyed much form, but he now unfurled strokes that remain etched in the memory of those who saw him that day. Passing fifty in 63 minutes, he treated pace and spin with similar disdain, his finest strokes hammered through the covers off front and back foot. Of all who were at Old Trafford that day, Raman was the one with a box seat view. 'He belted it beautifully,' he says. But where others might have been lured into trying to match Dexter's brilliance, Raman knew his role was to hold down an end. 'He has a shrewd cricketing brain,' wrote John Woodcock, 'as well as a calming influence upon others, and he played just the innings that was wanted of him.'

Twenty minutes before tea the score was 150 for one. England were ahead of the clock. Even Dexter's dismissal at this score could not derail them. Or so it seemed. The breakthrough came when Benaud, without a wicket in the match, found a thin edge as Dexter tried to cut a ball perhaps just too close to him. Two balls later, Benaud, now bowling round the wicket into the rough, struck again as May was bowled round his legs. Enter Close to play as reckless an innings as Test cricket has witnessed. Half a dozen ungainly heaves yielded one six before he was caught at backward square leg. England needed to regroup. But to the last ball before tea the man best placed to do it was out: Raman was yorked by Benaud for 49. For Alan Davidson this was

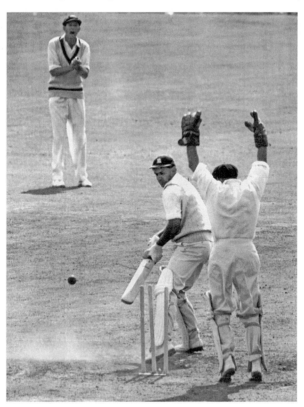

The turning point: Raman bowled by Richie Benaud for 49

the game's final twist: 'The moment Richie bowled Raman was the turning point.' The Australian captain had claimed four wickets for nine runs in 19 balls. England's hope now was to salvage a draw. It proved forlorn. With 20 minutes to spare, Australia had won by 54 runs. England, two matches to one down, could not retrieve the Ashes.

For Raman it was back to county cricket for what would be the last time. There were four matches – two losses and two draws – before the final Test. After the first of these, at Worcester, came the formal announcement of his retirement. He bade farewell to Northants with an undefeated 80 at Wellingborough in his last appearance in front of his home supporters before joining his England colleagues for the final Test. He had made plain that he would not take part in the final county games of what had been a sadly unsuccessful season.

Going to the Oval the England team had only pride for which to play. It started disappointingly. May won the toss, but with the Australian bowlers getting the early help he may have feared, his side was soon 20 for three, both openers and Cowdrey out. May and Barrington staged a recovery, but 256 was a score that Australia soon overhauled with centuries from Harvey and Burge. All out for 494, the tourists looked at the prospect of an innings victory. Rain helped England's cause as they strove to avoid defeat and 32 were added without loss on the Saturday evening. Resuming on Monday, Pullar immediately departed, Cowdrey failed for the second time and, though May helped Raman add 50, a duck for Dexter meant that, at 90 for four, it was a long haul ahead. Rain again lent a helping hand, but at the close Raman and Barrington were still together. At 155 for four, England were 83 behind. 'Only the incurable optimist can believe that Australia will not achieve their most conclusive victory of the series,' opined John Woodcock.

Next day proved one for the optimist, and Woodcock was able to report that Raman had concluded his Test career 'in romantic style'. His partnership with Barrington yielded 172 runs, but after reaching 95 Raman laboured for 16 overs. He remembers well the ball that brought up his century. 'I was on 99. Alan Davidson was bowling at the other end. As he passed me from short leg, he whispered, "For God's sake, Raman, don't get out!" He had had his squarish fine leg up for saving one, but he deliberately pushed him back so that I would get a single.' The ball Raman needed was delivered in his favourite area and tucked round the corner. 'Can you imagine that happening today?'

Raman progressed to 137. It took him six and a quarter hours and for most of his innings he had batted with a runner. By the time of his dismissal the match was still not safe, but Murray and Allen ensured that England would not lose. By scoring a century in his first and last Ashes Test Raman had emulated another fine left-hander, Maurice Leyland. His 468 runs in the series was the most by a batsman from either side, and with 46.80 he topped the England averages. He would go to Hastings in September to lead A.E.R. Gilligan's XI against the Australians then sign off with 60 as captain of an England XI against a Commonwealth XI. Thereafter club cricket beckoned.

Raman and Ken Barrington acknowledge applause as they return to the pavilion at lunch on the final day of the fifth Test. Raman's runner, Ted Dexter, is on the left in the background.

13

'If he'd have been skipper, I'd have gone like a shot!'

A career in perspective

Raman departed first-class cricket with over 14,000 runs averaging better than 41 with 30 hundreds, three of them in Tests, where his average was close to 47. To those who played alongside him in county cricket, especially in his later years, he was seen as a fine player, while Peter Arnold comments of his earlier days at Northants that 'we all said that as a cricketer he made the very best of his ability.' Adding that there were more natural players around, Peter sees as one of Raman's greatest strengths that 'he never gave his wicket away.' His strokes were usually said to be limited, Mick Norman listing them as 'the glance to fine leg, pulling the ball and a cut through the covers not unlike Alastair Cook's.' Mick had seen Raman club the ball over midwicket, but there were few of David Gower's languidly timed strokes and little was hit down the ground.

Somehow Raman lacked a hallmark stroke, for ever suffering from comparisons with Ted Dexter, and leaving as cerebral a bowler as Don Shepherd searching vainly to recall any special field placings he might have considered for him. To Mike Smith the single word 'sound' encapsulated Raman's batting, making him an ideal opener. 'Bags of determination, and courage too,' Doug Insole adds, a timely reminder that the first of Raman's three Test hundreds was made with a damaged hand and his last with a runner. Playing before the advent of one-day cricket, Raman's own philosophy, was always to build an innings in a manner the modern player often finds hard. 'There's no point in flashing around early on and getting out. You need to have a proper approach and get stuck in, get the feel of everything, the pace of the wicket, the bowling. Then you can start to be more liberal in what you do.' Yet *Wisden*, celebrating him as one of its five Cricketers of the Year for 1960, gives the lie to Raman's own modest assessment that he was 'pretty dreary' as a batsman. 'If anyone believes that batting is dull when he is at the crease, it is suggested that a closer inspection be made. Note particularly the times when he keeps pace with harder-hitting and more stylish players and his willingness to upset the field by going for sharply run singles.' A knack for finding the gaps ensured that Raman kept the scoreboard moving, the almanack went on to suggest. It was a knack well appreciated the following year by Alan Davidson, who opened the bowling to Raman and Pullar in all five Tests. 'He could play the ball to any part of the field. He never tried to overstretch. Some batsmen think they are pretty good and you play on their ego, but Raman was always in such control. A wonderful temperament.'

And what of his captaincy? His time leading Northants was never easy. Taking over from a popular and deeply respected captain, he was initially a victim of the high expectations of all at the Club. He had come in largely bereft of on-field captaincy credentials. Initially seen as slightly shy, he was reliant on the special mystique the amateur was expected to bring. Exercising his bridge brain, he relished the tactical challenges each match presented, but what had he particularly enjoyed about county captaincy? 'Such a lot of nice captains to deal with,' he replies, his answer redolent of an age now long passed. Yes, there were indeed many who would be friends for life. Peter May at Surrey, a man Raman had always liked from their Cambridge days, Donald Carr at Derbyshire, a godfather to Raman's son Alistair, John Warr and Robin Marlar, both captains of Cambridge teams in which he had played, Mike Smith at Warwickshire, with whom he shared a room on tour and who would ask Raman to be godfather to his son Neil, Colin Cowdrey, another known from university days and with whom he had toured.

With friendships stretching beyond the men involved, Anne teamed up with Mike Smith's wife Diana to scour the south coast for a holiday home by the sea. They found a bungalow at West Wittering that they bought together. Some years later it was demolished in favour of a house built on the same site. Delighted to find Diana preferring the upper floor of the new building, Anne owns the downstairs part of the house. The home is still shared by the two families with the Smiths' three children having taken over their late mother's share of the house.

These good friends from the Oxbridge fraternity of English cricket would assemble with others for Gentlemen and Players matches, representing a stratum of society that the structure of the game sought to protect. It was highlighted at some of the major grounds, where the two amateur captains were to be found in their own dressing room, their status further emphasised by a twelfth man instructed to tend to their every need. Back in 1950 Peter Arnold, already overcome by the whole experience of playing at Lord's, had his greatest surprise when summoned by the captains. 'I knocked on the door. Bill Edrich and Freddie Brown were in a dressing room as big as ours, just the two of them. "The steward knows what we want – a couple of double gins." It was eleven o'clock in the morning!' Times might have started to change by Raman's day, but for Mick Norman it still illustrated the divide that he should feel awe-struck in going to the captains' room at the Oval to take his cup of tea to England captain Peter May.

County cricket enjoyed a class-based structure that lay comfortably alongside the in-built traditions of life in the services with its commissioned and non-commissioned ranks and attendant protocols. 'When an officer told you to move, you moved,' says Malcolm Scott, recalling a banal truism of forces life familiar to all with experience of National Service. The memory has a particular salience for Malcolm, who was drafted into the RAF and did his 'square bashing' at Bridgnorth at the time Raman was serving there as a Pilot Officer. 'Don't say the Raff, it's the Royal Air Force, Malcolm,' he remembers Raman remonstrating. And as he relates the story Malcolm's Geordie twang gives way to the received pronunciation of the English gentry. He draws a parallel between the barrack room of his service days and the Northants dressing room. 'Stepping into the second team never mind the first, it was like back in the forces, all the different dialects.' It had started with Australians, then all Ken Turner's recruits from the Minor Counties, notably Staffordshire and the North East. 'What did he say?' a Geordie might ask when a Black Country team-mate spoke.

Then, as the youth of the day was finally excused the need to serve two years in uniform, the in-built disciplines began to ease. By 1960 the likes of Colin Milburn were arriving at Northampton without the rough edges knocked off. 'Some pipsqueak telling you you didn't bowl so well,' Malcolm remembers one colleague complaining. If respect was in shorter supply, the scramble for places in the county second eleven was not. The success of Ken Turner's football pool led Northants to opt for a larger staff than most of the counties. It meant that places in the second team were at a premium. 'You could make 60 or 70 and it would be "Have a rest for the next game."' Never mind the crowded dressing room, 'The Hut', where the second team – and those not yet established in the first eleven – all changed, the need to fight for a place bred an attitude of selfishness. Malcolm Scott came well prepared. He had played for Durham and for the Minor Counties representative side, and in his formative years he had come briefly under the wing of Alec Coxon, as tough a competitor as ever played for Yorkshire. 'Play for your bloody self' was his advice to a young Malcolm.

Those whom he led have been quick to talk of Raman's educational background, sharply different from most in this rough-edged dressing room. When first appointed he could be likened to the callow junior officer still needing to prove himself to battle-hardened men more inclined to listen to a long-serving sergeant, but by the end of his time he had become more akin to a war hero, a man to whom most of his team instinctively looked up. For a cricket-mad youngster like Brian Crump, the son of a successful league professional, who from childhood had bowled at his younger cousin David

Steele on the specially prepared strip in the back yard of their grandparents' home, to bat alongside an England player was the consummation of his adolescent dreams. 'I always enjoyed batting with Raman,' he says. 'Very gentlemanly the way he talked to you between overs. Nowadays they don't seem to chat – they just punch! It was bits of advice – "Take your time, don't rush it." Or when a new bowler was coming on, "This chap bowls away swingers." Little things all the time, giving you encouragement. Brilliant!'

Likewise for Mick Norman, whose talent was released under Raman, memories are wholly positive. 'A splendid captain,' he says, going on to relate how Raman once restored his sagging morale. 'I had been having a lean spell and I thought my number might be up and I'd find my name missing from the team sheet. Raman saw me in the bar looking gloomy and he came up to me and said, "Are you OK, Micky? Worried about anything?" I told him I was worried about my form. He said, "We're not going to drop you. You save me 15 runs an innings. You can add that to the runs you make." It was a huge weight off my shoulders. It gave me a bit of confidence and put me on the road back.'

As a leader Raman was never flamboyant. That wasn't his style. Clapping of the hands and 'C'mon, chaps' is Malcolm Scott's image, and it compares favourably with others from the amateur side of the divide. Fellows-Smith, given a few chances to impress in the second eleven, is remembered as one too quick to bellow, while the successful years of the quietly determined Keith Andrew are seen in sharp contrast to the over-assertive manner of Roger Prideaux, insensitively bawling out his players in public. Even the sergeant major approach favoured by Brian Reynolds as senior professional cost him friends, whereas his ready smile and softly spoken encouragement brought Raman respect whatever the on-field fortunes.

Illustrating the see-saw nature of fortunes in county cricket, only four years after Raman's team had finished just one place from bottom, Northants were denied the title by four points. Their own programme completed, the players had anxiously awaited the outcome of Worcestershire's match against Hampshire at Bournemouth. Northants sat at the head of the table, but they could not afford for Worcestershire to win. Telephone calls kept them in touch, bringing news of a rain-affected match in which both captains, in search of ten points for a win, declared, Hampshire once the follow on was saved, Worcestershire after one ball of their second innings. Colin Ingleby-Mackenzie, underestimating the malevolence of a drying pitch, had thought 147 in 140 minutes within the compass of his batsmen. When Hampshire were bowled out for 31, they could congratulate the new champions. But did they spare a tear for Keith Andrew and his men?

For Northants it was still a transformation of fortunes, and one for which Andrew must be accorded great credit. He had been appointed captain on the back of a pair of wins at the end of the 1961 season after Raman had called it a day with the county. Those two victories had lifted Northants off the bottom of the table amid great celebration. Had there not been this final upturn to the season, there would have been an untried amateur in charge in 1962. Roger Prideaux, with no prospect of captaincy at Cowdrey's Kent, was joining as assistant secretary in time for the season, his playing talent crucial to the appointment – and, as with Raman, at least the implication that he would captain the team. This final fling for the amateur or shamateur would have cost the county the services of their wicket-keeper, who saw the captaincy as the new challenge he needed to extend his career. For Andrew things soon started to look up – his side rose to eighth place in his first year. Apart from a surprise call up for a single Test in 1963, he could devote himself full-time to his county as Raman seldom could, and the pool of talent on which he could draw was growing. Since Raman's time, Milburn had established himself, while Prideaux, David Steele and Haydn Sully had all arrived, but with Crump, Larter and Scott the principal wicket takers and Jim Watts and Reynolds the leading run-makers, there had been a flowering of seeds sown under Raman.

Raman's decision to pursue a full-time business career came when his international stock was at its highest. Had he remained in cricket where might the game have taken him? He was turning his back on a tour of India at a time when both May and Cowdrey had announced that business priorities would keep them at home. When a list was published with 24 players who had indicated their availability to tour, there were other major players unavailable, while there was still uncertainty about whether Dexter would tour. In the end it was Dexter who would lead the party with Smith as his vice-captain, but Raman had been vice-captain ahead of both in the West Indies, and Peter May had gone out of his way to persuade him that he should make himself available to lead the side. 'I still wish he had gone,' says Anne, her view reinforced by her own love affair with India.

The initial list of 24 had included the two youngsters from Raman's Northants who had done most to fill the breach in a disappointing season, David Larter and Brian Crump. Larter's time would come the following summer, while Crump, fearing for how his constitution would stand up to months of curries, confesses that he had hoped that when the final party was announced his name would not be there. It wasn't, but told that Raman might have been persuaded to captain the side he now says, 'If he'd been skipper, I'd have gone like a shot!'

14

'Tremendously enthusiastic about everything he did'

A proper job and back to club cricket

On 7 March 1961 Raman and Anne's first child, Christopher, was born. In December the following year their daughter Michelle was born. In 1965 there would be a second son, Alistair. Raman was now feeling the responsibilities of being a family man. It had helped confirm his feeling that he had been right to make a break from cricket when he did and settle down to a conventional job. Despite his original intention to pursue a career that would make use of his law degree as a company secretary, Raman had found his metier in the world of publicity working for Noel Gay. In 1962 he moved on to W.S. Crawford, one of London's major advertising agencies, for whom he worked in their public relations subsidiary. There his most significant work was to help British apple growers make the most of their wide range of products. At a time of heavy advertising for French Golden Delicious, home growers lacked any unified approach to promote their own produce. 'It was all pretty shambolic,' Raman explains. 'The farmers all went off and did their own thing, not at all to their benefit.' What it needed was coordination – a favourite word of Raman's that would soon be applied to English cricket. 'We brought the whole thing together. We set up a company to control the whole business and got someone in to run it.' Home Grown Fruits, as the company was styled, remained a client of Raman's for many years after he had set up his own consultancy, Management Public Relations Ltd., in 1969. Another loyal client was the Brick Development Association, whose need was to persuade architects of the merits of brick at a time when buildings of plate glass and steel were becoming fashionable.

In deciding to set up the new company Raman approached two colleagues with whom he had worked at Crawford's, Michael Cornish and Felicity Rutland, to join him as co-directors. Cornish had, by this time, moved to S.H. Benson, a one-time giant of the London advertising scene, and he was delighted to escape from what he now describes as 'the Titanic'. The new company was soon thriving. In their premises in Blackfriars the three founder directors shared an office, unusual practice at the time, enabling all to have a feel for what was going on with each other's clients. 'We always trusted each other,' Michael Cornish stresses as he describes the rows they could have – nearly always about what was best for their clients. Over its years in operation until Raman was the first to retire in 1992, the company remained small, with no more than three or four staff, preferring to outsource for the services they required rather than carry the overheads of a design studio and similar facilities.

Michael Cornish remains a lifelong friend. He recalls Raman fondly, coming to work in all weathers without an overcoat, favouring instead large woolly sweaters. 'He was never a snappy dresser,' he says, but it was an age of formality with suit and tie de rigueur and Cornish comments that it was not long before you knew a man's life history once you had decoded his school, university and services ties. He looks back on an age where business practices were not shaped by today's technology and the mobile phone was science fiction. Advertising and PR agencies were boltholes to which client personnel would sneak away from their offices with an at least plausible pretence of being about some pressing business, and the certainty, if they played their cards right, that they would be entertained. 'I remember a dreadful little man from the Brick Association,' says Cornish, 'a chain smoker – and Raman hated smoke – who used to come at 5.15 on a Friday afternoon. He had to be offered a drink and he would sit there until after eight.'

Michael never ceased to admire Raman's dedication to his job. 'He was always very charming and friendly at all levels. And he always seemed to be tremendously enthusiastic about everything he did.' Another of Raman's traits, much admired by his friend, was his ability to address awkward topics, where there was a need to persuade a client to act against his natural instincts – to adopt a hitherto alien course of action or not pursue a particular pet project. 'And when he had convinced them, he was able to make them think it was their own idea, when it wasn't!'

His enthusiasm for their business made Raman popular with clients, who always felt they were getting more than a full share of his time, though in reality it only happened because he was always prepared to work extra hours to compensate for what became his first priority, the work he was doing for cricket and, especially, Surrey County Cricket Club, who billed the firm to enable Raman to devote long hours to work that might otherwise have been undertaken by a paid chief executive as he strove to put the club on a sounder financial footing.

As cricket began to dominate Raman's working life, Cornish recalls one man who was always popping in, and from his description it was plainly Donald Carr. But with another cricket contact Cornish has no identity problem. He speaks of the endless telephone calls from South Africa. Adopting a stage-perfect South African accent, he mimics the voice of Ali Bacher. 'Is Raman there?' I know he's there. I can hear his voice!' Raman became one of

English cricket's principal links with South Africa as he maintained low key contact with Bacher, a man who worked tirelessly to sustain and integrate his country's cricket, while Raman waited patiently for the day when the TCCB would need to be ready for a South African team to be re-admitted to the international fold. There was a particular poignancy for Raman in all he did, knowing that South Africa was a country around which he could never have hoped to travel freely. 'I couldn't go. I had a British passport, but they would have known the Indian connections and in those old-fashioned days you had to keep out of certain areas, which was awful.'

Though in no sense a close follower of cricket, Michael Cornish was able to see the fruits of Raman's efforts for the game, and he could empathise with Raman battling to convince an army of die-hards that there was money to be made from advertising at their grounds. 'He never sought to make a penny for himself,' Cornish stresses, going on to speak in glowing terms of Raman's ground-breaking initiatives such as persuading BT to operate a service providing up-to-date scores from all the county grounds. 'It brought a lot of money into the game, but he never looked for two per cent for himself.'

Still a young man when he retired from the first-class game, Raman was determined to continue playing cricket when he could. He had always remained involved with the Old Whitgiftians, playing some mid-week and Saturday games with former pupils of his old school during his early vacations from Cambridge. At this time the Old Whitgiftians did not play cricket on Sundays, but as more clubs and villages began to do so, a group of Old Whitgiftians and others formed an informal wandering side to enjoy some Sunday games. Playing under the name of The Casuals and fixing up matches with local clubs, the team was often captained by Raman's brother Stanley, a slow bowler and useful club cricket batsman.

John Webb, captain of Whitgift in 1956, whose mother was later to accompany Raman's mother to the Oval, recalls playing in some of the matches for both the Old Whitgiftians and The Casuals while still in his early teens. He remembers that Raman's father, 'a charming gentleman,' often came to watch. Stanley, as captain, always took pains to put the younger players at their ease, and the young Webb looks back, too, on the thrill of batting alongside a Cambridge Blue. He speaks of the encouragement Raman gave to the younger players when he played. 'We once put on a hundred together,' Webb says, and so unassuming and lacking in self-importance did he find his partner that it came as a surprise that Raman, a quintessential amateur, should end up playing in the professional game of county cricket.

Raman's brother Stanley

With matches for the Stoics and a few MCC games as well, Raman was never short of cricket. It was to become easier still for him to play locally in 1965 when he heard of a house for sale looking over the Old Whitgiftians' ground. Raman and Anne could not believe their luck when they were able to purchase the home in which they still live. To reach the ground over the past fifty years Raman has had only to walk through his back garden and onto the outfield. He has a grandstand view of the cricket if he chooses to take a deck chair onto the lawn in summer. And if he prefers to watch from under cover he has only to look out of the back window of his living room.

In the early 1960s club cricket in most of the south of England was played on a purely friendly basis. Indeed membership of the Club Cricket Conference was not open to clubs that participated in league cricket. Exemplifying the forward thinking for which Raman was to earn a reputation, he began to feel that much of the social cricket he was playing was just too casual. Players turned up late and the result was almost immaterial provided a good time was had by all with a few beers afterwards. 'We enjoyed the spirit in which we played our cricket,' he said at the time, 'but we felt this spirit could be retained with an edge given to the cricket at the same time.'

The driving force behind the idea of bringing league cricket to Surrey, Raman found like-minded club captains in other clubs. Fearing that if they did not act an outside body might try to impose a less palatable structure on local club cricket, he called a meeting in the Old Whitgiftians' clubhouse after the 1966 season at which he outlined his thoughts to representatives of 21 clubs. He found more support from players than from administrators who had retired from playing the game, and further objections were encountered from the Club Cricket Conference, but the prevailing mood was with Raman. In the 1968 season the Surrey Championship was launched.

Despite poor weather that summer the new league flourished, as a report in *The Cricketer* by Norman Parks of Beddington makes clear: 'The majority of players involved enjoyed playing competitive cricket. There was certainly more bite to the game, and the players were more enthusiastic as also were the supporters. The general standard of the fielding was certainly improved. There was some dull negative cricket, but this was outweighed by some very positive play.' There had been some initial dissenters, but it was not long before they found their best players drifting towards the Surrey Championship. 'It didn't take long for them to change their minds,' says Raman and the league that was his brainchild fifty years ago now has a reputation as one of the country's strongest with Old Whitgiftians yet to grace the recently named Premier Division but holding a mid-table position in Division One since 2010. The success of the Surrey Championship is widely acknowledged as helping to spread league cricket across the southern half of the country.

Raman continued playing cricket until well into his forties, still retaining a particular affection for the Stoics, of whom he is now a vice-president. His own memory of the Stoics and how they operated was that everything was run from The Crown in Brewer Street in London's West End, where Vinty Bromage was the landlord. In fact, the club was founded in 1877 to play mid-week matches against the strongest clubs in London and the Home Counties. The Stoics' special place in history is as the opponents in the field for six and a quarter hours at Hampstead while one-time England captain Andrew Stoddart made 485 in 1886. His score and that of his team, 813, were both at the time world records. And why did Hampstead not declare? Because they were not allowed to!

It is believed that this match hastened the passing of a law three years later to permit an innings to be terminated before all the batmen were dismissed. Those who fielded that day at Hampstead may have felt themselves doubly qualified to be called Stoics, a label that is earned by displaying 'self-control, fortitude and detachment from distracting emotions, sometimes interpreted as an indifference to pleasure or pain.' The definition concludes that 'it allows one to become a clear thinker, level-headed and unbiased.' Just what Raman was to become in cricket administration! In 1897 the Stoics elected Stoddart as their president, hardly an honour likely to be bestowed today on a captain exercising the right he still has to bat all day in a traditional declaration match.

The club made its first overseas tour in 2008, visiting Sri Lanka when Raman also happened to be on holiday on the island. With members across the globe, the Stoics team when Raman met up with them in Kandy included Test cricketers Aamir Sohail of Pakistan and Danny Morrison from New Zealand.

Raman at Kandy with a picture of Stoics president
Gerald Plumley, a member of the club for 70 years

15

'A most imaginative, far-seeing mind'

On the Surrey committee

Cricket has always been central to Raman's life, and it was not long after his retirement from the first-class game that he was back at the centre of affairs. A Surrey man from birth and with his home in South Croydon, it was inevitable that his loyalty would be to his first county, where he had scores of friends, many now in influential positions. Elected to the county committee at the Oval in 1964, he was embarking on a career of service that would see him play a crucial role in rescuing not only Surrey but the wider first-class game from the verge of bankruptcy, eventually setting it on the road to the thriving multi-format sport it has become.

Around the committee table at the Oval he found men steeped in devotion to cricket and its traditions but loath to address the underlying problems that beset a first-class game that was destined to become progressively less sustainable without new sources of finance. In addressing these problems Surrey were soon to become a trailblazer for the counties. For this they were indebted not only to Raman but also to another Surrey supporter who was to become a staunch friend, Bernie Coleman. Now in his nineties, Coleman looks back on a life where his business interests suffered from his devotion to the cause of cricket. As a self-confessed cricket nut, he has no regrets. 'I have enjoyed every minute of it' he says. His involvement began in the late 1950s, and he was first persuaded to stand for the Surrey committee by Stuart Surridge and Peter May. As a man whose living came from owning a small string of pubs, built up from taking over The Castle in Tooting Broadway from his father shortly after the War, he was stepping into unfamiliar territory. The committee he was joining seemed overstocked with those who had titles inherited or earned in fields unconnected with cricket. 'People said, "What's this publican doing on the committee?" Stuart said, "He might help us to make some money."' So began an involvement with the game that started with Coleman enquiring whether any rent was charged to the pub at the entrance to the ground and finding that it contributed nothing.

Working in unison, Raman and Coleman became instrumental in formalising the role of marketing. With a committee of 24 elected members as well those holding ex officio positions, there was no shortage of personnel round the table, but they were distributed across just three sub-committees responsible for: finance & general purposes, cricket and house. There was no formal role for marketing, no commercial cutting edge to what was going on. Raman and Coleman soon began to effect change, and in 1967 Surrey became the first county to embrace marketing matters within its committee structure. Initially there was a public relations sub-committee with Raman as chairman with a separate sales promotion sub-committee chaired by Coleman, on which Raman also served. In 1969 the two sub-committees were merged with Raman as chairman and Coleman a key member, as he would continue to be into the 1990s, when his long years of service were crowned with the presidency of the county.

Derek Newton, later to become chairman of the club for 15 years, was another soon involved. He had first encountered Raman when he had written to ask if his Old Emmanuel club might be represented at the first exploratory meeting at the Old Whitgiftians Club in Raman's quest to set up the Surrey Championship. A friendship developed and Newton was soon invited to bring his considerable management skills onto the county committee. A long-serving member of Raman's sub-committee, later to take its chair, he saw Raman and Coleman working together at close quarters. With a future treasurer Peter Wreford, they would later be branded 'the gang of four'. Newton describes how they worked: 'Raman had a most imaginative mind, a far-seeing mind. He had ideas and he fitted in beautifully with Bernie Coleman. I have to say that Bernie was probably even more futuristic than Raman. As a team they would chat together regularly. They came up with the ideas. Peter Wreford and I were good doers. But Raman also had the ability to get on with it.'

Coleman has no doubts about the part that Raman played. 'He was a great visionary at a time when the game was flat broke.' A visionary – it is a strong word, and one that Coleman has chosen carefully. He applies it also to Geoffrey Howard, the county's secretary between 1965 and 1974. Howard had been assistant to Brian Castor at the Oval until he left for Lancashire in 1949. A measure of Surrey's problems lay in his comment that on his return he could find 'no perceptible changes at all at the Oval.' Speaking of his other visionary, Coleman says: 'Raman was like a beacon of fresh air when he came on the committee. He was a very discerning man and he was a clear thinker. He could see long before anyone else what was needed.'

Moreover, perhaps unusual in a conceptual thinker, Coleman saw Raman as strong on detail. 'He was so thorough in everything he did. Everything had to be correct. I didn't have such a tidy mind.' Together they set about bringing money into the county club. An early step was to exploit the opportunities for advertising on the ground, which they realised would shoot up in value with exposure to the television cameras. But they had first to suffer an apoplectic reaction from Gubby Allen, whom they struggled to pacify with assurances that the Excess Insurance hoarding beside the score box was a significant money earner. 'I told him it was bringing us £500. Mind you, Gubby was God,' Coleman explains. 'He ran the MCC and he ran cricket, and no-one dared argue with him.' Fortunately for Raman and his friend Gubby Allen did not run Surrey.

By this time Raman had been elected to the MCC committee and over the next two decades and more he would be serving the cause of both Surrey and the wider world of cricket, most especially in his roles with the shortly-to-be-formed TCCB. But this is for a later chapter. Concentrating on his work with Surrey, the 1968 Year Book found him explaining to members what the new marketing team were up to and the problems they faced. Gate receipts were down from £28,000 in the late 1950s to £8,000 with an inevitable rise in subscriptions. Signing up advertisers had been an obvious source of revenue, if revolutionary at the time, but other initiatives were also under way. Sponsors were found for matches. A membership drive was launched, and season ticket holders, previously stigmatised by a name that was redolent of British Rail, became the Surrey Taverners with their own stand and bar. A company privilege scheme was launched to nurture corporate support. A more vigorous and coordinated approach to junior cricket in the county was adopted. All this activity justified the recruitment of a full-time sales promotion officer, John Shoobridge being appointed to the post.

A great ideas man, Coleman brought a pop concert to the Oval in 1971. There were 40,000 people and just one policeman, he remembers. Among those providing the entertainment were The Who and a more recently formed group The Faces, for whom Rod Stewart was lead vocalist. The event made almost £5,000 for the county club. The next year saw Ladbroke's betting facilities on the ground, while money also came in from such diverse attractions as Sunday markets, Christmas funfairs and donkey derbies.

Meanwhile Raman, prepared to grasp nettles where needed, set out to dismantle the cumbersome committee structure at the Oval. Coleman recalls that it was Raman who tactfully persuaded Maurice Allom that it was time for him to retire as chairman, a post he had held since 1966 when the president of the day, Lord Nugent, had first suggested that it should no longer be combined with the presidency. At the same time Raman made it equally clear that there was a need for a treasurer attuned to modern thinking, Lord Ebbisham stepping down in favour of Peter Wreford. In 1974, after management consultants from Cooper Brothers had been brought in, a new structure was in place with Raman as chairman of an executive committee comprising just ten people. Among those on this new slimmed down body were the key figures of Bernie Coleman and Derek Newton.

It was not all plain sailing. At the end of the 1974 season Geoffrey Howard had retired. He had always been attuned to new thinking, which had warmed the hearts of the younger element on the committee. Howard's successor was of a different mould. He came straight from an army posting in Northern Ireland, and he arrived with the rank of Lieutenant-Colonel. If there was a caricature of a county secretary of that era it might well have been a man retired from the services. Indeed, Howard's predecessor and assistant had conformed to this image, being nicknamed 'the Army and Navy Club'. Warren Sillitoe was initially told he should drop the title, but once in post he chose not to do so. It was symptomatic of the attitude of a man who was never going to be attuned to the thinking of Raman and his commercially-oriented colleagues. His three-year stint came to an end shortly after the fondly remembered Sir George Edwards, famed aircraft designer and soon to be president of the county, strolled round the ground with him at Guildford. At the end of their circuit Sillitoe tendered his resignation. Not long after he was to die tragically in a road accident.

In the mid-1970s Surrey's on-field fortunes had slumped. Champions as recently as 1971 and second two years later, the county had a membership conditioned to expect better than 14th place in 1977, Sillitoe's final year, and the penultimate spot twelve months later. It was at this point, in October 1978, that Sillitoe chose to offer his views on the county's demise to *The Sunday Times*. He took the chance to point the gun firmly at Raman, linking his name with those of Newton, Coleman and Wreford in branding them 'a caucus of four that dominates the committee.' They were taken to task for 'running the club as a business' and Raman was taxed for ignoring recommendations of the consultants by denying Sillitoe a chief executive role, while he and his three close colleagues made all the executive decisions. In siding with the members, who had been understandably concerned at what had gone wrong on the pitch, he painted the committee as too distant from the members and players. 'At social functions,' he wrote, 'they seem to drink, talk and leave together as a group.'

The departure of Sillitoe brought in a structure wherein the new secretary, Ian Scott-Browne, had none of his predecessor's pretensions to a chief executive role. Instead, Raman effectively took on the mantle himself. His colleagues recognized that this could never be practical so long as he remained an unpaid volunteer. An arrangement was therefore reached whereby Raman's time was invoiced to his company, where his devotion to the cause of Surrey cricket was to become a dominant memory of his colleague Michael Cornish.

In his role as chairman of the executive committee he was soon working ever closer with Derek Newton, who looks back in some bewilderment that his own employers in the insurance world should so freely spare their chief executive. 'It could never happen today,' he reflects.

Coming from a man who, Raman and his colleagues had concluded, was not up to the job, Sillitoe's strictures may seem harsh, but the playing performance of the county team was an understandable cause for concern. In 1971 Micky Stewart had fulfilled his ambition in winning the Championship by a whisker from Warwickshire. It should have been a fitting close to his career, but he was persuaded to remain for another, less happy year before passing the captaincy on to John Edrich, who never relished the job. There had been several unfortunate losses of players, the first coming when Bob Willis, though an England player, was expected to remain with Surrey on second team wages. By 1972 he had moved to Warwickshire. Then, after the 1975 season, wicket-keeper Arnold Long left the Oval for Sussex, to be followed by England pace bowler Geoff Arnold two years later, while all-rounder Stuart Storey, who had retired from Surrey in 1974, also emerged at Sussex in the same season as Arnold. For 1978 a new captain, Roger Knight, had been lured from Sussex to preside over a discontented dressing room. His arrival coincided with the last of two seasons served by Fred Titmus as head coach. With a year of his contract still to run, Titmus left the Oval, recognising that his heart lay north of the river. His time with Surrey had coincided with the two most disastrous seasons in the county's history.

Whatever the criticisms of the disaffected former secretary, Raman soon proved himself able to address them. On Boxing Day 1978 Micky Stewart made his way through the snow to Raman's home. Derek Newton was also there to discuss the possibility of Stewart returning to the Oval as cricket manager. They found unanimity in discussing the role. Stewart did not wish to be just a coach and selector for the first eleven; he also wanted to be responsible for developing cricket across the county. So began the restoration of Surrey's fortunes. In 1979 the county finished third in the Championship. The following year they were runners-up to Middlesex.

While Coleman had been principally responsible for many of the early revenue-earning ideas, it was Raman to whom thanks were due a few years later for a brilliant money-saving initiative. It had come as a major blow to learn that the perimeter wall at the Oval had to be replaced. The council had decreed that it had become unsafe: replacement was the only option. Derek Newton puts it all into context. 'Although today Surrey is the wealthiest club in the country, in those days (early 1980s) we were the one closest to going to the wall because we had the same crowds as, say, Derby and Northants, but

Raman presents a model of a new stand

we had enormous expenses.' There was, of course, an appeal to the members to pay for a new wall; but the few hundred pounds this brought in did not begin to address the problem with a bill of around a million pounds expected. 'We put our heads together,' says Newton, 'Raman said, "I reckon I could do a deal with one of my clients."' Reminded of this, Raman waves his hand in the direction of the fine brick fireplace that is a feature of his South Croydon home. He had earlier explained that this had been a gift of his client, the Brick Development Association. Now he recalls how his client answered his call for help with the wall. Not only would there be a generous deal on the bricks, but the labour would be provided at no cost to Surrey, coming as part of a formal training scheme for apprentice bricklayers. 'It was built for a tenth of the real cost,' says Derek Newton.

Never frightened to step into uncharted waters, in 1980 Coleman was behind the first floodlit cricket match in England. His plan was for Surrey to play a West Indies team at Stamford Bridge, but success in the Gillette Cup made it impossible for the Surrey players, so Essex, who had been considering a similar venture at Chelmsford, stepped in. Around 15,000 spectators, among them Mick Jagger who had flown in from Paris, saw Graham Gooch hit ten sixes in a match finally curtailed by persistent rain. The same format at Ashton Gate in Bristol brought almost 8,000 to witness Ian Botham lead an England team against the Rest of the World. With a profit of £25,000 on the night from his Chelsea venture, Coleman was delighted with everything he saw. Admitting that the night would 'make the purists at Lord's shudder,' Alan Lee in the *Evening News* reported that 'the event attracted an audience and match action quite divorced from first-class cricket – and, to have any future, night games must be viewed in that way.' Raman and Bernie were ahead of their time as ever. Day-night cricket eventually overcame objections that it could never work in England, while it would be 23 years before the ideal format of Twenty20 matches was implemented, notwithstanding suggestions from Peter Lush at the TCCB that appropriate games could be fitted into the summer programme with inter-city contests mooted at this early stage.

Perhaps the most ground-breaking of all the ideas Coleman and Raman hatched together came to fruition in 1989, when it was suggested that the ground might be branded. Now common practice around the sporting world, it was dismissed as pie in the sky when Coleman first mooted the idea. He remembers going to the London flat of Bob Cowper, the former Australian Test cricketer, who was then representing an Australian brewing concern in the UK. There he met Cowper's Australian boss and discussion turned to the challenge of promoting a brand of lager, until recently available only in cans, but now on draught in the UK, the first market in which it was offered in this form. Might the amber nectar not gain added momentum from a plug with every media mention of The Foster's Oval? Coleman's idea struck a chord. But could it happen? The Surrey committee, of course, raised questions about venturing into such unknown territory. 'There's a ground across London,' the quick-thinking Coleman replied, 'named after a man who had been a wine merchant among his other wheelings and dealings.' A deal was struck that was eventually to bring Surrey £4 million, making possible the building of the Barrington Indoor School and much else.

It was not long before Cowper introduced Coleman to the man in whose business empire the original parent company of Foster's lay. John Elliott, a controversial figure in Australian business and politics, had a passion for Australian Rules football, the club of which he was president carrying the name of his Carlton Brewery. Elliott worked into the naming deal a provision that there should be an annual Australian Rules match at the Oval. There had been one such venture a few years earlier, but since that time a change of head groundsman had brought the legendary Harry Brind to the Oval.

It fell to Raman to break the news of the forthcoming match to Brind. 'I recall Raman taking him out for a beer or 27,' Derek Newton quips. 'The following night Raman had to take him out again because he had forgotten to tell him that he wouldn't even be able to cover up the Test match pitch!' Despite the invasion of the square the Oval's growing reputation for producing some of the best batting pitches in the country remained undamaged as spectators gathered to witness this antipodean game on the ground where England's first soccer match, against Scotland, had taken place in 1870. Typifying the resistance that was to be expected with any novel initiative, the whole idea of meddling with the name was anathema to a section of the members. 'They were very cross,' Newton recalls. 'They called a special meeting, but they lost.'

The Queen with Bernie Coleman
followed by Prince Philip, Alec Bedser and Derek Newton

16

'It was all a bit hit and miss before'

From MCC to TCCB

While he remained heavily involved at the Oval, Raman had also been making waves on the national scene. In 1967 he was elected to the MCC committee. With Peter May and Dennis Silk, he represented a new generation serving on a body at that time charged with overseeing the welfare of the domestic game at all levels. Dominating deliberations at his early meetings was the thorny question of how best to ensure that a tour to South Africa would take place as planned during the winter of 1968/69. Raman heard the rival arguments aired. Denis Howell, recently installed as the country's first Minister of Sport, had made plain his preference for seeking positive assurances from South Africa, whereas Sir Alec Douglas-Home, an immediate past president of MCC, drawing on his experience as foreign secretary, persuaded the committee that it would be better to allow matters to take their natural course rather than force the issue. The ultimate clumsiness of what became the d'Oliveira affair was duly recorded in the minutes. The tour was called off once objections were raised to a man of colour in the MCC party, after which the focus switched to making preparations for the reciprocal tour scheduled for 1970, where Raman would play a more important role.

Alongside such discussions committee agenda were fattened by less weighty items redolent of MCC's traditional values. Thus the committee ensured that Wilfred Rhodes' ninetieth birthday would not pass unacknowledged, but they regretted that it was deemed inappropriate for the ashes of S.F. Barnes to be scattered at Lord's. In some ways it all had a reassuring and gentlemanly cosines, and this extended to the international scene where the ICC (at that time still the Imperial Cricket Conference) had always been run from Lord's with the club's president, for his single year in office, acting as chairman, while the Secretary of MCC performed the same role for ICC, providing the continuity no chairman could.

On the domestic front, until the abolition of the amateur and the introduction of a limited overs knock-out competition for the 1963 season, there had been few disruptions to the format and character of the domestic game since the 19th century. But change was on the horizon – and it was needed. Whereas the crowds had flocked to watch county cricket in the early post-war years, by the 1960s a competition with professional teams playing six days a week throughout the summer was no longer viable.

Addressing the game's financial perils was now the key to all that began to happen. Hitherto £6,000 had been extracted from Gillette to attach their name to the new one-day competition. 'At least it was a start' Raman concedes, but it had been a pretty timid one that reflected the limited commercial acumen of those running the game. MCC had earned a reputation for commissioning enquiries and watering down any radical recommendations, but there were modest stirrings in the wake of the Clark Report of 1966 to suggest that this one might have more impact. Among its main recommendations had been easing the passage of overseas stars into the county game, which came about in 1968, and introducing a 16-match one-day league, which happened in 1969. The report also proposed undertaking an examination of commercial sponsorship. A final recommendation was that someone be appointed to look after press and public relations. Jack Bailey, a former Oxford Blue and Essex player, was identified as the man for the position and was appointed in 1967. For Lord's it was a first toe into the water of modern marketing methods, and he would find Raman at his side in his marketing endeavours.

The arrival of Bailey at MCC soon caused ripples. Once in post, he made his mark by shaking up the comfortable relationship with the BBC, whereby the broadcaster had always paid what it said it could afford to provide television coverage of Test cricket, each year proposing a figure to which MCC politely acquiesced. For the 1968 Gillette Cup Bailey opened negotiations more widely. The contract was duly awarded to ITV, only to have the broadcaster cut away from an exciting final as the penultimate over approached. Had five more minutes been allowed, viewers would have seen Alan Smith ride his luck in taking his Warwickshire side to a four-wicket victory over Sussex. But obligations to advertisers and rigid inflexibility in the screening time for subsequent programmes left millions still wondering half an hour later how the match had finished – with many indignantly blaming MCC for the fiasco.

These were among the last initiatives Bailey would be taking in which he would be wholly answerable to MCC. The governance of domestic cricket, since time immemorial the exclusive preserve of MCC, was about to be wrested from the club's grip. The catalyst for this came from a government initiative that began to make public money available for leisure activities with the Sports Council, now Sport England, set up to administer grants. While other sporting bodies were starting to reap benefits, no funding from the public purse would find its way to cricket if it had to be handed over to a private club, which MCC clearly was. Raman was a member of the small sub-committee given the task of recommending a new structure for running the domestic game. He was enthusiastic for change. 'It was all a bit hit and miss before,' he says. 'I realised, sitting on the MCC committee, that the whole thing needed re-shaping. There was a huge job to be done.' Raman was aware of unease among the counties, most notably Lancashire, around this time. He saw a danger of a hostile breakaway – 'people going off doing their own thing, which would have been disastrous.' He saw a continued role for MCC, but not running the whole show and now leaving the commercial aspect to others.

The sub-committee's proposal was a first step in the direction Raman felt the game needed to move. It saw the creation of a Cricket Council with three constituent bodies: the Test and County Cricket Board (TCCB), responsible for the first-class game; the National Cricket Association (NCA), taking on the mantle of what had been the MCC Cricket Association and looking after the recreational side; and MCC itself. It was the beginning of a process that would end with a game more professionally run, immeasurably sounder financially and with the best performers eventually reaping rewards that meant that cricketers would no longer be the poor relations among top sportsmen. It was a process with which Raman would be closely involved for more than 20 years. It would give rein to his visionary qualities, but it would not be achieved without hard fought battles and some acrimony along the way.

The inaugural meeting of the Cricket Council took place on 22 January 1969. 'An important milestone in cricket' it may have been for *The Times*, but the new structure was initially little more than cosmetic. The Secretary of MCC, Billy Griffith, assumed the same role with both the Cricket Council and TCCB. All bodies were housed in the pavilion at Lord's with MCC stationery freely used for communication, while MCC's assistant secretaries provided all the necessary administration. Moreover, the composition of the new bodies resulted in the familiar names of the great and the good at MCC emerging under new hats. Initially MCC was the dominant member on the Cricket Council with eleven voting members (including Raman) against ten for the NCA and only six for the TCCB, though their number already included big hitters such as David Clark, Wilf Wooller and Doug Insole. To the left-wing writer Mike Marqusee the aim behind the reconstruction of the governing body was 'not to replace but to retain the old order.'

Was this so surprising? After all, where were other people to be found who would know more about running the game? And many of the same mundane operational tasks still had to be performed: drawing up the fixture list; getting tickets printed for Test matches; appointing umpires to first-class matches and scrutinising their expense claims. To the public there was precious little to tell them that anything had changed let alone cause them any concern. They would see England teams continue to tour under the banner of MCC until 1976/77 and retain MCC's overseas colours for another 20 years. Small wonder that confusion reigned and for several years MCC became accustomed to taking the flak for what were often TCCB decisions.

There was, however, one area where life was emphatically different. Raman now had a more fertile base from which to operate as he became chairman of a public relations and promotions sub-committee. Before long marketing terminology, about as alien as an open neck shirt in the pavilion, was being heard within its confines as Raman and his cohorts began sparking life into the commercial side of the game. The formation of Raman's sub-committee, an extension of an endeavour he had started within MCC, provided a logical base for Bailey as its paid administrator. For him it was an almost seamless change in function.

Raman was now in his element, no longer restrained by MCC's traditional conservatism as he embarked on a long period of service to the Board, culminating in taking the chair in 1985. From the outset he made sure that commercially-minded people were brought in, one of the first his friend Bernie Coleman, who would succeed Raman as chairman of the marketing committee five years later and serve in the role for 18 years. Mike Turner, who had proven himself a dynamic secretary at Leicestershire, and Derrick Robins, chairman of Banbury Buildings, who had been an influential figure at Warwickshire and Coventry City Football Club, were two others bringing talents not readily found at MCC.

Bailey grew to know Raman well. Like Michael Cornish, he respected his capacity for hard work and visionary qualities, while he was never fooled by Raman's gentlemanly exterior, writing that 'beneath a warm and friendly exterior there lurked a certain ruthlessness.' An early success came as Raman and his committee supported Bailey in a tactic of extreme brinkmanship. Convinced that the BBC were getting Test cricket on the cheap, they determined to hold out for a greatly increased fee for televising the summer's Test matches against West Indies. It was a nail-biting time for all as they refused to back down in MCC's time-honoured manner, knowing that the BBC faced the risk of *Radio Times* going to print while still unable to promise viewers television coverage of the Test matches. The stakes were high on both sides, but using their PR skills, Raman and Bailey had won the support of the counties. They were all rewarded when the telephone rang in Bailey's office as the deadline approached. In that instant the BBC had become the beggars, enabling MCC to rake in a fee double that of earlier years.

As with so much at MCC, those running the game had been slow to exploit the potential of one-day cricket. Notwithstanding the crowds attracted to the Gillette matches, the limited overs format was still too readily trivialised with establishment voices decrying any departure from traditional on-field tactics, the notion of saving runs taking precedence over taking wickets offensive to their sensibilities. It was also still an age where county cricketers were expected to play two three-day matches most weeks, with Sunday as their one day off; but a tradition had grown up whereby many of the players' cherished Sabbaths were devoted to playing games in aid of a colleague whose benefit year it was. This long-established practice had attracted the attention of the cigarette company Rothmans, who had seen an opportunity to recruit a team of international stars styled the Cavaliers to play against one of the counties in front of the cameras each Sunday. The success of these matches, both in attendances at the grounds and, more pertinently, in attracting a television audience helped confirm Raman's belief that a Sunday League was exactly what county cricket needed.

Six years had been allowed to pass before this second one-day competition was up and running. Now it came with a season-long impact. Plans for the Sunday League had been formulated in the months before TCCB was set up, and it was an immediate hot potato for Raman's new committee. Some problems were known: the Sunday Observance Laws initially made it impractical to charge for entry, usually overcome by selling programmes, while 40 overs became the maximum length of an innings as games were forbidden to start before 2.00 pm. Moreover, the players' participation – essentially denying them their one day off in the week – rested on enforcing their terms of employment. It also meant that it was no longer possible for stars contracted to a county to opt for the rewards offered by Rothmans, and the Cavaliers matches did not long survive.

These were the days when sport was freely sponsored by tobacco companies just denied the right to advertise their cigarettes on television – and many players enjoyed the free products on offer. So John Player of Nottingham was signed up as sponsor for the Sunday League, the £75,000 fee extracted emphasising the low price Gillette had been asked to pay only six years earlier. Bernie Coleman well remembers joining the committee and learning of the problems of ensuring television coverage of the games. It all came hot on the heels of the ITV fiasco with the Gillette Cup final, which had not prevented the independent contractor maintaining it held an option on that competition for future years. This in turn cut across the BBC's bargaining stance in which their negotiators sought to link coverage of the Sunday matches to restoration of their right to the Gillette Cup. Fortunately for all concerned at TCCB, when ITV took the matter to court, the contractors' case found no favour with the judge.

Three years later the age of smoke-filled rooms saw another tobacco brand, Benson & Hedges, linked to a third one-day competition. This time the company paid £65,000 with £15,000 in incentives to the players. In the same year Prudential were persuaded to lend their name to a series of three one-day international matches against Australia, the first to take place in England. The Prudential Trophy would run for a further ten seasons and the company's name would also be linked with three World Cups staged in England.

Perimeter advertising was introduced to the Test grounds. A new TCCB magazine was launched. As time went by MCC's priorities were not always in harmony with the TCCB's new initiatives and single-minded determination to make money, but Bernie Coleman looks back with few regrets: 'What we had to do was drag people into the twentieth century. There were constant rows with the BBC about money, but all the chairmen of the counties I got on very well with because they knew I was making them money. Anything I put forward, they always supported.' It wasn't quite so easy with Gubby Allen and others at MCC obsessed with more traditional values, but Raman

Raman pioneering a new commercialism

never lost his focus: 'He was always talking about the future of the game and how things should be done,' says Coleman.

Battles lay ahead, but before differences became apparent and relationships strained, there was much to keep all parties united. South Africa were due to tour England in 1970. Guided by the principle of fostering cricket wherever it was played, the establishment view, expressed formally by the Cricket Council, was that the tour must go ahead. Such a view was in no sense condoning apartheid but it recognized that the South African Cricket Board had to operate within the laws of their country. There was, however, significant opposition to the tour from within the game voiced by such figures as David Sheppard and Mike Brearley, whose answer to a country imposing such an inhumane regime was to starve it of all sporting contact. It wasn't just a battle of words. A more militant 'Stop the Seventy Tour' campaign, headed by a youthful Peter Hain, then a student at London University, was set on disruption of the matches.

Though a strong police presence had enabled rugby matches against South Africa to go ahead, it was obvious that the task of defending all the county grounds would prove impossible, so plans were made for a shortened tour with only twelve matches, all to be played on the major grounds, where there was some prospect of defending playing areas from the actions of determined saboteurs. Raman was clear where he stood on the issue, having earlier been a spokesman in support of Dennis Silk at MCC's 1969 AGM when a motion to end cricket contacts with South Africa was overwhelmingly rejected. His company was now engaged in a professional capacity at Bailey's instigation to bring Raman's skills to the dissemination of information that would help to keep the tour on track. It was never going to be an easy matter. Though opinion polls showed the public in favour of the tour, Harold Wilson's Labour government was unequivocal in hoping to see it cancelled, though with a General Election in the offing, government ministers still preferred to declare it a matter on which it was for the cricket authorities to take the decision.

Raman and Bailey trod a careful path, issuing a statement after the Cricket Council's initial decision, in which they were at pains to 'repeat their aversion to racial discrimination of any kind' and 'respect the rights of those who wish to demonstrate peacefully.' But they made their position crystal clear: 'Equally they are unanimous in their resolve to uphold the rights of individuals in this country to take part in lawful pursuits, particularly where these pursuits have the support of the majority.'

Among more mundane activities with which Raman and Bailey busied themselves was leafleting those attending the rugby matches, while one of the major challenges they faced was in deciding how to respond to a broadcast by the prime minister in which Harold Wilson, speaking on the *Sportsnight* programme, had told the nation that it should feel free to demonstrate at any of the tourists' matches. The press looked to Bailey for a response but he was unable to reach his superiors to sanction the wording of a statement, Billy Griffith having apparently taken his telephone off the hook. It was Raman who persuaded Bailey that they must act. Together they drafted a statement which was released to the Press Association. Bailey's recollection of what was said is reproduced from his book *Conflicts in Cricket*:

> 'In his broadcast this evening, the Prime Minister referred to the right of all people to demonstrate freely during cricket matches against the South Africans this summer. He has also mentioned that the Cricket Council should not feel that they were being blackmailed.
>
> It is for the Prime Minister to decide whether incitement to demonstrate constitutes blackmail, just as it is for the government to decide whether law and order can be maintained in the face of demonstrations.
>
> If for these or any other reasons the Prime Minister feels that the tour by the South Africans should not go ahead, then he should come out and say so, to the South African government.'

The wording is a masterpiece of the public relations art. What could the government say in response? There were countless meetings and representations made to the cricket authorities, with the threat of a boycott of the Olympic Games by black nations from Africa, but the Cricket Council held firm in maintaining a stance that both condemned apartheid and supported the continuing of sporting contact between the two countries. A 1970 Tour Fund was launched with the twin aims of helping to meet the extra costs of providing security for the tour and furthering the objectives of multi-racial cricket in South Africa.

Eventually the government's bluff was almost called. It became increasingly apparent that the tour would be beset by problems that would render the matches almost impossible to be played. The final decision to call off the tour came from the Cricket Council, but they acted only after extracting a formal request to do so from the home secretary. Raman was among many saddened that so many fine cricketers were to be isolated from the international game.

All change or no change?

MCC's committee room at Lord's, the venue for a Cricket Council meeting
in 1970, where many of those round the table will have gathered for meetings
of MCC's own committees. Raman, at 38 the youngest in the room,
sits at the far table with Jack Bailey and Donald Carr to his right.

17

'Jack wouldn't accept that the game was run by TCCB'

The battle for control at Lord's

In the early years of the new structure for administering cricket most things happened as they always had done, if with a bit more commercial tinsel. However, Raman first ruffled feathers at Lord's in 1972. At a time when MCC still dominated the Cricket Council, he was a member of the Council's own Reorganisation sub-committee. His experience with Surrey had taught him to be wary of complex committee formality. He felt that change was called for and spent two and a half hours trying to convince his colleagues that management consultants should be called in to make recommendations on how the Council should be structured. He failed to persuade them. Nor did they take his point that it was undesirable for the Secretary of MCC to act at the same time as chief executive of the Council. In the end Raman walked out of the meeting, resigning from the sub-committee. He later expressed his concern that MCC should wish to have 'as many fingers in as many pies as possible.' He had been elected a member of MCC in 1955 and throughout his years with TCCB his affection for the club never wavered, but he felt it was bad for the game that the new committees should not be able to develop in their own way.

He also feared that someone less sympathetic to MCC might wish to see TCCB sever all connections with Lord's, which he felt would be a pity. He was aware of the ambitions of Cedric Rhoades, who had taken no prisoners in winning the chairmanship at Lancashire, where he had help lift the county from a prolonged spell in the doldrums. Now Rhoades was throwing his weight around in TCCB, proposing that it should break away with its own small secretariat – and a wage bill clipped to £5,200! He saw Nottingham, with its good motorway accessibility, as an ideal base. Eventually management consultants were brought in and as a result the influence of MCC was reduced to give the club five votes in the Cricket Council, equal to those of each of the other two bodies, TCCB and NCA. On top of this was a change of chairman. Hitherto the Council chair had always been taken by the incumbent president of MCC with the vice-chairmanship in the hands of the Treasurer of MCC, the all-powerful Gubby Allen. From 1974 the Council's chairman would be elected for a term of five years.

These changes coincided with Billy Griffith's retirement as Secretary of MCC. No longer were two of MCC's assistant secretaries to devote a majority of their time to TCCB affairs. Instead, Donald Carr came off MCC's payroll and was wholly responsible for TCCB affairs as its secretary, while Jack Bailey was appointed Griffith's successor at MCC. Commentators have suggested that the two men were assigned to the wrong jobs, and this is certainly Bernie Coleman's view. He saw Carr as the comfortable traditionalist happy to go with the flow, while Bailey was the more commercially alert of the pair. These appointments helped to emphasise that, despite initial appearances, the functions of MCC and TCCB were importantly different, and this would soon become ever more apparent.

As a consequence of the changes another vacancy arose on the permanent staff for what was described as 'Secretary Public Relations for MCC, the Cricket Council and the TCCB'. There were early hopes that Raman might take the job, but he preferred to retain the freedom to continue working in the public relations business he had started only five years earlier, and he was not keen on the proposed reporting structure. If the title of the new job at Lord's suggested some residual confusion about who was running cricket, it attracted plenty of applicants before the appointment of Peter Lush was confirmed. Hitherto a director of an advertising agency – he had known Anne Subba Row at Ogilvy and Mather – Lush won the job after a daunting interview in which he had faced at least seven of cricket's hierarchy across the committee room table at Lord's, Raman among them, though the president, Lord Caccia, and Gubby Allen fired most of the questions.

In all practical senses Lush was working only for the TCCB. Bailey's elevation to take over from Griffith meant that his work for TCCB ended abruptly, and his single-minded priority from now on would be the welfare of MCC. 'When I arrived hoping for a handover briefing and so forth, he had nothing to do with me at all,' Lush now says, commenting that he soon saw Bailey's attitude cool towards Carr. It could be said that battle lines were being drawn up. 'Jack wouldn't accept that overall the game was run by TCCB. That was the nub of the matter,' says Lush.

At the heart of arguments that lay ahead was the core remit of each organisation: the MCC secretariat and committee were answerable to their members for the maintenance and running of what was their ground, whereas TCCB's priority was the financial welfare of the first-class game and the performance of England teams. MCC's priorities were spiced with concerns for the good of the game and its almost mystical values, whereas for TCCB ensuring that it had a sound financial base was paramount.

Raman had played a crucial role in setting the whole marketing movement on its way at Lord's, but he now made way for Coleman as chairman of the sub-committee, allowing him to devote more time to affairs at the Oval. It was with Coleman that Lush would principally work, and work harmoniously with great mutual respect, into the 1990s. They came together as money was beginning to flow into the game in a way never considered feasible a decade earlier. But more needed to be done, and Lush was quick to address the pricing of tickets for Test matches. It wasn't always easy. 'I got objections from Gubby Allen, who seemed to be opposed to anything that needed modernising and changing.'

One matter that had been barely addressed was the way the players were paid. This was to be a big help to the Australian media mogul Kerry Packer, when he found his efforts to win the television rights to his country's Test cricket falling on deaf ears at the Australian Cricket Board. The rewards he was able to dangle before the world's leading stars took care of any recruitment problems he may have had when he planned to stage his World Series matches in opposition to official Tests.

The Packer affair, as it has become widely labelled, had the effect of thrusting MCC into the limelight as the club's secretary and president, donning their ICC hats, summoned urgent meetings of the other Test-playing nations. The TCCB and ICC were at one in doing all they could to sustain official cricket in the face of Packer's threat, denying his matches first-class status and decreeing that any player making himself available for a match disapproved by the Conference (as Packer's clearly were) would thereafter be ineligible to play in any official Test match. This attempt to defend the official game was challenged in the High Court, where Packer won an injunction to prevent the rule being implemented. With the case generating a bill for £250,000 to be shared out and with legal advice that an appeal was unlikely to succeed, there were those at the TCCB who wondered at the wisdom of fighting over what was always primarily a quarrel between the Australian Board and an Australian broadcaster. Surrey had stood apart from those determined to fight on at all cost, and Raman was certainly one who favoured a rapprochement with Packer, most particularly because he wished to see Packer's money channelled into the game as a whole rather lining the pockets of a privileged few.

Raman's stance was evidenced as early as February 1978, when he wrote to *The Times* endorsing their cricket correspondent's suggestion of getting round the table to thrash out a formula for cooperation. 'I may sound like a hawk transformed into a dove,' John Woodcock had written in proposing the thought that Packer might be offered sponsorship and television rights to a one-day competition. Woodcock had been to the Sydney Showground to see for himself the new form of cricket on offer to the Australian public, and he came away appalled by 'the indiscriminate use of bouncers and all the razzamatazz'. Raman wrote, as chairman of Surrey, stressing his county's loyalty to TCCB, but going on to say: 'We believe that a round-table meeting would enable each side to analyse the good and the bad elements of both systems and could even lead to a unification of the two – for the benefit of the game, the players and the watching public the world over.' Raman's call was not in tune with the English cricket establishment. His letter drew forth a reply from the man who had kept wicket for Cambridge in Raman's first season, Oliver Popplewell QC, destined to become a high court judge and president of MCC. 'Beware the siren voice of compromise,' he counselled.

Eventually the Australian Board came to an agreement with Packer, perhaps best described as a climb-down, and the circus was disbanded, but not before it had had its impact on how cricket would be played in the future. Such features of the modern limited overs game as day-night matches, white balls, coloured clothing, universal helmets and fielding circles were spawned or encouraged by the Packer circus. So, too, was an intensity of competition that sprang from a gladiatorial style of promotion that found expression in increasingly uncouth player behaviour. All this would have its impact in later years for Raman as an international match referee, but the most immediate consequence was the need for more money to be found to ensure that England's players would henceforth be substantially better rewarded and less readily tempted to follow whoever might pop up next with sacks full of dollars.

This was the moment at which the cricket-following public was first made aware of an insurance company called Cornhill. Needing to build the brand awareness from which confidence flows in insurance circles, the hitherto little-known company ploughed an annual £200,000 into the five years from 1978 to become cricket's first million pound sponsor. For this sum new ground was broken as the summer's Test matches were allowed to be prefixed by the Cornhill name. With this went extensive advertising rights at the Test grounds, while the company was also given entertainment facilities that meant many of the boxes at Lord's were starting to house more folk escaping the office for a jolly and fewer true cricket buffs. The new money brought into the game also meant that England's Test players were enjoying greatly improved pay. Before Packer an England player received £200 as his fee for a Test match appearance. This modest reward leapt to £1,000 in 1978 and continued to rise until the Professional Cricketers Association expressed concern that there was an unreasonable gap between the Test player and the county stalwart.

Sponsorship also came to the County Championship with Schweppes the first company to lend its name to cricket's premier domestic competition. Starting in 1977, the company remained loyal for seven years before making way for Brittanic Assurance, whose name branded the Championship for the next 15 years. Meanwhile Gillette had been superseded by NatWest for the principal one-day knock-out competition. 'I sacked Gillette,' says Bernie Coleman with a broad smile, recalling how the razor blade manufacturer had thought £30,000 enough to hold onto the sponsorship when the bank were willing to pay £100,000. Keeping sponsors sweet and giving them value for money was central to the marketing effort at the TCCB. But this could only be achieved if TCCB could offer relevant incentives and make promises to those who were pouring their money into the game. It meant that counties whose grounds were staging international matches found themselves required to bend to the wishes of the TCCB, making space for sponsors' advertisements and giving up seats for their guests. This had been a gripe in Warren Sillitoe's attack on Raman and his colleagues at the Oval.

Though all the counties stood to benefit from TCCB's endeavours, the demands imposed upon those staging the major matches were seen at their most intense at Lord's. MCC provided TCCB with its home base, and though it enjoyed a share of the overall takings, MCC soon found its ground being treated as though it belonged to the TCCB. Ask the average spectator in the Mound Stand who he thinks is running the show he has paid his money to watch and he may look blank. But behind the scenes there have been years of wrangling over such issues as: who prices the tickets; who keeps the money brought in; who decides that there will be reduced prices when an early finish looks likely on the final day; who fixes all the advertising; who is responsible for public announcements; whose remit includes ground security; who should introduce the players to the sovereign – the president of MCC or the chairman of the TCCB? The list of issues with potential for pre-match bickering is endless, and the sparring began in earnest at the time that Raman, Bernie Coleman, Peter Lush and others were striving to put cricket on the road to prosperity.

TCCB was to usurp more power as the years passed, and an important attempt to accelerate the trend came about in 1978. In that year a working party of three was set up by the TCCB to examine, and make recommendations for improving, the governance of cricket. The group's chairman was Raman. Working with him were Cedric Rhoades and Ossie Wheatley, a former Cambridge Blue and captain of Glamorgan. They spent six months interviewing members of the various bodies. Their view was that there was a clear need to streamline decision-making. In passing they regarded the NCA as doing a good job, but saw no merit in giving money to the Minor Counties, who contributed little to the prosperity of the game further up the chain. Most crucially, they said of MCC that its contribution 'cannot be significant to either the professional or amateur game.' They saw neither an administrative nor a financial role for the club. Their key recommendation was to do away with the Cricket Council, creating instead a United Kingdom Board of Control on which the 17 first-class counties would be dominant with eight places given to the NCA including a lone voice from the Minor Counties and there would be just one place for MCC as guardians of the Laws. This board was to meet twice a year while the engine room would be manned by an executive committee meeting every six to eight weeks and comprising a chairman, five representatives of the first-class counties, three from the NCA and four chairmen of subcommittees whose areas of responsibility would be cricket, amateur, finance and marketing.

Though the proposals anticipated much of what would characterise the present England and Wales Cricket Board (ECB) even more feathers were ruffled at MCC, while there was no united view from the counties with one submission dubbing the triumvirate 'the three blind mice'. Turned down by 16 – 4 in the Council, the ideas advanced by the threesome inspired a more palatable alternative from a group led by Mike Turner that still pursued the goal of giving TCCB greater control of the professional game. Eventually, in 1982, a structure emerged in which there were to be eight TCCB votes in the Cricket Council against five for the NCA but just three for MCC. In the event of MCC and NCA ganging up on TCCB, the TCCB would still prevail by now holding the chair. The resignation of Gubby Allen ensued, though he was soon to become a more influential figure within TCCB, his eligibility to stand for any position with MCC having been lost when a new ruling was adopted that those who had passed their seventieth birthday might not stand for election to office at MCC.

There was scant immediate reward for the three who had wished to see more radical changes imposed on English cricket. Rhoades was becoming something of an outsider, respected for what he had achieved at Old Trafford but too determined to sweep the old establishment from the scene and seeking to impose a playing structure that would bring an end to the conventional 17-county competitions. He did not gain a place on the executive committee at the TCCB in 1980. Nor was Raman elected, both he and Rhoades retaining their positions at the TCCB by virtue of sub-committee office and through representing their respective counties. However, whatever his position, Raman was still well placed to maintain influence on affairs through his friend Bernie Coleman, who was now at the peak of his powers on the marketing committee. But for the winter of 1981/82 Raman would be away from his London desk, a different challenge awaiting him as he accepted the offer to return to his beloved India as manager of the England team.

18

'I reckon he was glad to see the back of me'

India with Fletcher – and Boycott

'Lord's had a brainwave.' Thus John Woodcock gave his verdict in *The Times* on the mid-August appointment of Raman as manager of the England team to tour India during the winter of 1981/82, supporting his assertion by describing Raman as 'a very good player in his day, with a close understanding of the modern game and the patience needed for an Indian tour.' There was reference to 'a determined streak behind his gentle nature' before the assurance that 'the touring team will like him for his fairness and respect his ability as a player; the Indians will like him for his quiet style.' Raman was at this time devoting much of his time to affairs at the Oval, where he was chairman of the cricket committee and executive deputy chairman of the club. He would soon become more deeply embroiled with affairs at TCCB, but it was a moment when he could make the time to take on the job in India.

Raman had visited India three times since his trip with the Commonwealth side, but management of a full England tour almost 30 years later brought his first chance of spending most of an English winter in the homeland of his father. A tour planned to stretch from early November to late February was to include six Tests with three ODIs threaded into an 18-match programme in India; then five games were to follow in Sri Lanka, two of them ODIs and one a Test to celebrate the host country's admission as a full member of the ICC. It was a hectic schedule, but the tour was keenly awaited in India, with England's stock high having just retained the Ashes in dramatic fashion in what will always be remembered as Botham's summer.

Ian Botham, soon to be restored as a national hero, had cut a sorry figure leaving the crease at Lord's having completed a pair in what was to end as a drawn match. But the loss of the one-day series and the first of the season's six Tests at Trent Bridge following a drubbing in the Caribbean meant that questions were being asked of Botham's right to a place in the side, let alone the captaincy. His resignation that evening at Lord's brought former skipper Mike Brearley back from international retirement. Whether by inspiration or just good luck England's restored captain appeared to have a magic touch at crucial moments in the subsequent matches, but it was Botham's heroics at Headingley, Edgbaston and Old Trafford that played the key part in the destiny of the series.

With Brearley now making plain that his return to the captaincy was only for the summer, the selectors had to cast their net elsewhere for the demanding tour of India. They settled upon Keith Fletcher, a batsman who had played the last of his 52 Tests four years earlier. A good player of spin bowling with two previous tours of India and an impressive record as captain of Essex, he had much to commend him. The team he led had Botham, David Gower and Graham Gooch near the peak of their powers, but the party contained some players who had passed their prime. Vice-captain Bob Willis was beginning to feel the strain of more than a decade spearheading the attack, opening batsman Geoff Boycott and wicket-keeper Bob Taylor were both over 40 while Derek Underwood, at 36, was embarking on what would be the last series of his metronomic left-arm spin. Others in the party still had much to prove and some would never make their mark as Test cricketers.

For all the keen anticipation of the series ahead on the sub-continent, the whole venture had hung in the balance only days before the tourists were scheduled to depart. The ban on South Africa's participation in international cricket (and many other sports) brought implications for those who set foot in the country whatever their motive. The previous winter had seen the Jackman affair, whereby the Surrey bowler's call to reinforce the England side on tour in the West Indies had caused a Test match to be moved away from Guyana. Robin Jackman's Test debut came in Barbados, where a more liberal attitude to his having played for Western Province and Rhodesia prevailed. But it had been a close call with the risk of the tour being aborted. So it was again as the England party had wondered whether they would ever board their plane for India. The problem players now were Boycott, who had coached in South Africa while on holiday, and Geoff Cook, the Northants opening batsman, who had played and coached more extensively across the racial divide.

Raman waited patiently as George Mann and Donald Carr, chairman and secretary of TCCB, were advised that it would be fruitless for them to embark on a diplomatic mission to meet with the Indian Board. The decision was for the politicians, they were told. Mrs Gandhi, the prime minister, kept her counsel but appeared to be requiring the omission of Boycott and Cook from the party. Such demands would have led to the abandonment of the tour. Cook, a surprise choice for the tour, made a suitable statement, but Boycott proved more problematic. It was at this juncture that Raman's old friend Robin Marlar received a surprise call from a high-ranking official in the Indian foreign office. The official had read his articles in *The Hindu* and believed he was the man to unlock the problem of Boycott. Could he go round to the Indian High Commission that afternoon where a meeting was taking place? There Marlar found Mann and Carr, but it was at his suggestion that a call was put through to Boycott's hotel in Hong Kong. A long and tortuous conversation took place in which Boycott's wish to tour was clearer than his other utterances. 'I can tell by that telephone call,' said the High Commissioner, 'that he's a very awkward character. We can't allow an awkward character to wreck the tour!' Eventually hearing the players' suitably disapproving comments of the apartheid movement, Mrs Gandhi felt able to take a more magnanimous attitude. So, to the joy of India's cricket-mad public, the tour proceeded – and the Indian prime minister was able to take credit for it doing so. As, in a lower key, could Robin Marlar.

The pattern of matches across the tour was in sharp contrast to those of the modern era, where three clear days must now be allowed between Test matches and where ODIs are held as separate series, usually involving many players not considered for Test cricket. For Fletcher's side there was seldom more than a single day for travel between matches, and there were some hairy moments with the arrangements. No sooner had the party arrived at Bombay than Raman was engaged in diplomatic negotiations over the supposed agreement for a package of charter flights for three planned journeys. The TCCB believed they had negotiated a price of £3,000 with Indian Airlines, only for Raman to find local officials starting to do their sums and realising that there had been rises in fuel costs and that each charter journey would involve a return trip with a potentially empty plane. Suddenly £12,000 became the price to which Raman was expected to agree.

The plan had been for charter flights to be taken on a Monday from Poona, where the second match of the tour was to be played, to Nagpur, where the tourists were to meet the Board of Control President's XI. Then, after playing on Tuesday, Wednesday and Thursday, the team were to be flown on the Friday to Baroda for a match scheduled to start on the Maharajah's ground the next day. Without air flights there would be some uncomfortably long journeys, if no compromise could be reached. 'To have fares quadrupled is rather disappointing,' was Raman's masterly understatement as he considered the option of asking for the Nagpur match to be dropped altogether.

On the playing side the tour began positively. A one-day match was won at the Brabourne Stadium. This was then followed by triumph on the travel front that typified an Indian solution to bureaucracy. Faced with a train journey to Poona starting at the uncomfortable hour of 6.45 am, the team found travel agents able to book them onto an afternoon departure. This was no ordinary booking of rail seats as tickets were rationed to four per person, a problem the travel firm overcame by sending nine employees to queue at the station to procure all the seats the cricketers and the media entourage required.

At Poona a match of three declarations saw the England batsmen sweep to a six-wicket win against an Under 22 XI, after which, travel obstacles having been overcome thanks to Raman taking a tough stand with the airline, a strong Board President's XI was beaten by five wickets at Nagpur, with Underwood taking eleven wickets. Against West Zone on the Maharajah's ground at Baroda the England side were able to declare twice, losing only six wickets in the match, before the home batsmen held out for a draw.

The pre-Test games ended with a One Day International at Ahmedabad, the first ever on Indian soil. Today's ODIs are played to agreed ICC regulations, but the Ahmedabad match had been preceded by lengthy negotiations between Raman and the Indian Board. With quickly fading light always a consideration, Raman had preferred to play 45-over matches. In deferring to the host's preference for 50 overs, the agreed arrangement was that the first innings should end at the stipulated time for lunch and that the fielding side should then face as many overs as they had managed to bowl. Raman had hoped in vain to see some fielding restrictions, while he was also uncomfortable about the idea of a single interval to be taken between innings. Now common practice in the English domestic game, it was not so at the time. Breaks for lunch and tea were what the England players had grown used to and Raman had felt they would be especially disadvantaged by long fielding sessions in the Indian heat. The joker in the hands of the Indian negotiators was the already agreed and publicised television and radio schedules.

Raman was described as 'the diplomat supreme', a soubriquet the cynics might say he had earned by giving way to every Indian demand. 'We put our point of view forward to the Indian Board,' he later said, determined to damp down internal moaning. 'But at the end of the day we are playing in India and we have to do as the Board says.' The match duly proceeded bringing the England team a fourth victory in five matches. The bowlers never let India's batsmen break free, a final total of 156 for seven from 46 overs seeming well within their batsmen's compass. At 61 for four the game looked wide open, but Fletcher, Gatting and Botham sealed victory by five wickets with 13 balls to spare.

There was just a single day after their triumph at Ahmedabad for travel and settling in back in Bombay before the first Test at the Wankhede. The mood was optimistic. Most of the principal batsmen had decent scores under their belts, and if the quicker bowlers had struggled for success, Underwood had confirmed his ability to offer his captain a measure of control whatever the conditions. Tony Greig's team had won a series in India just five years before. Why should this buoyant England side not win again?

Today's Tests in India play to sparsely filled stands. Despite the passion for cricket, evidenced in the multitude of games, official and unofficial, across Bombay's Maidan, it is now only the shortest forms that bring in large crowds. The growth of television and a strangely bureaucratic attitude to the selling of tickets may have contributed to the decline in spectators at modern Tests, but back in the days when Raman was managing England the major grounds were always jam-packed, with the latest technology of the day – transistor radios – fuelling the passion for India's success.

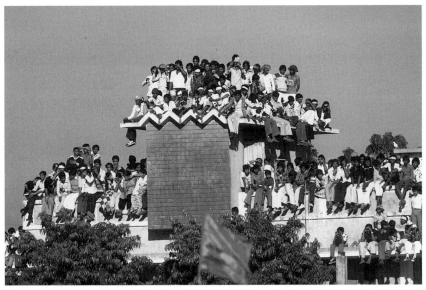

Spectators outside the ground for the one-day international at Ahmedabad

Sunil Gavaskar won the toss for India and chose to bat. With four wickets apiece for Botham and Graham Dilley, India were bowled out on the first day for 179. It had been a hard grind, but progress the next day was even slower. Having lost Gooch overnight, Boycott and Chris Tavaré added 92 in 59 overs. It was supposed to be the bridgehead for more positive strokeplay down the order, but it was not to be. The dismissal of Boycott heralded a phase of play that was to determine the outcome of the match and, ultimately, the series. A tight run out decision against Gower was followed by five overs from Dilip Doshi in which the left-arm spinner took four wickets for nine runs. The obdurate Chris Tavaré was caught at square leg, but Doshi's other victims, Fletcher, Botham and John Emburey, all returned to the pavilion feeling they had grounds for complaint about the decisions they had received, two lbws and one catch.

The expected lead did not materialise. By the close England were all out for 166. Next day the Indians batted just a bit more positively to end on 203 for nine, their lead now 216. The rest day was taken with England still having every hope that their batsmen could win the match. It was at this juncture that Raman made a bold move. He called an unofficial press conference at which he told reporters that the England team were dissatisfied with the standard of the umpiring. 'I remember saying we can't do it after the match,' he says. 'If we're going to do it, let's do it now.' He chose this moment so that, should England go on to lose, he could less easily be accused of pointing to the umpiring as the reason for defeat.

When the match resumed, it was not long before the ground was a blaze of firecrackers. England, finally set 241 to win, capsized tamely, a stand of 27 for the last wicket the highest of the innings as they were all out for 102. Raman now made his formal complaint about the standard of umpiring to the Indian Board. In his official release he said: 'Having advised the Indian Board of Control for Cricket prior to the first Test match that the England party were unhappy at the overall standard of umpiring, we have had a meeting today with the IBCC to say that in our view too many mistakes were made in this Test match. There are no complaints in respect of partiality.' Adding that he feared for possible damage to the good relations between the two sides if the matter were not addressed, Raman did not convince the Indian Board of his point of view. A lack of specific instances to support his contentions led to a rejection of the complaint, though different umpires were appointed for the next Test. Raman's principal target had never been the portly Swaroop Krishan, whom the England management had identified as the best of a not very impressive batch of officials so far encountered and who was later to be brought in to the third Test when an objection to a different official was more sympathetically heard. The man towards whom the dressing room oaths had been directed at the Wankhede was Komandur Ramaswami. He was to appear once more in the final ODI.

Always the visionary in challenging cricket's rituals, Raman was one of the earliest administrators to press for neutral umpires in Test cricket. His experience in India strengthened his conviction that this was an essential move for the ICC to take. 'That's the way the game had to go. The game off the field was becoming very much more of a business than ever before, and we had to have proper business rules.' With the passing of the years he has had time to reflect. Was it just incompetence his side suffered in India or did the England team suspect bias? 'Without being too diplomatic, I would say it was a bit of both,' he ventures.

After losing the first Test precious little went right for the tourists. The remaining five matches in the series were played out as the dullest of draws, the last two ODIs were both lost and none of the zonal matches that interspersed the internationals looked like achieving a result other than a draw. Underlying the problem were lifeless pitches, but the crucial factor in the Tests was that India, having taken a lead in the series, had no incentive to open a game up or take risks of any kind. Everything happened at a leisurely pace. India's overs through the series were bowled at 14.1 to the hour, while England, more reliant on pace with Emburey partnering Underwood in only three of the matches, contrived to be even slower at 13.26. The requirement to bowl a minimum number of overs in a day lay in the future, this series helping to advance the cause. It was another issue that exasperated Raman with the way the international game was run. 'We had to go through this awful boring period when things weren't happening.'

There were appropriate landmarks along the way, mostly marking the tedium of the play. At Bangalore in the second Test, Gavaskar, in taking 429 minutes to make 172, passed his century in what is today the third slowest time recorded for his country. At New Delhi Boycott contrived to bat even more slowly in completing his twenty-second and last hundred for England. At Madras Gundappa Viswanath and Yashpal Sharma batted throughout the second day but added only 217 runs. A declaration well into the third day had effectively killed that match before a sparkling century from Gooch brought a rare injection of life to the proceedings. His partner Tavaré, with 35 in five and a half hours, more aptly caught the prevailing mood. In the Tests it was rare for a match to progress far beyond one innings a side. Only at Calcutta was a challenge thrown down. An England declaration set India to make 306 in just over a full day's play, but a combination of mist and pedantic umpiring combined to reduce the playing time and only three wickets were captured as the match petered out with joke bowling.

If the matches were characterised by negativity, for Raman the series was punctuated by incidents that called for managerial intervention. At Bangalore Fletcher, a known walker in English cricket but one less trusting of overseas umpires, was judged to have gloved a ball to the wicket-keeper. The appeal had been far from full-throated and universal but it was enough for the umpire to raise his finger. As he departed the pitch, shortly to throw his bat at the dressing room wall, Fletcher wafted it casually in passing the stumps at the bowler's end. It was enough to disturb the bails and leave the off stump in need of straightening. It had not been a violent act and it had not provoked

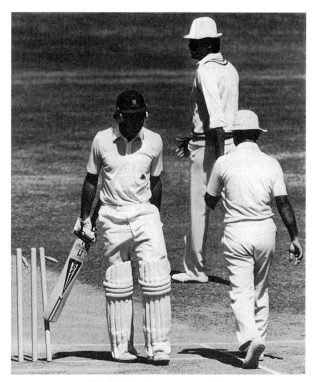

Keith Fletcher at Bangalore

a reaction from the Indian fielders, but it did not look good coming as it did from an England captain. Raman's instinct was to avoid escalating the situation. 'It was an instinctive gesture of disappointment at being out and not one of dissent,' he said. 'If all the stumps had been knocked flat it would be a different thing.' For Richard Streeton, reporting the tour for *The Times*, the image of English cricket had been tarnished, while a contrite Fletcher himself admitted that he would have admonished an Essex player acting in such a manner, and he sent a letter of apology to the president of the Indian Board. The whole incident nevertheless served to fuel English suspicions that they were getting a raw deal from the Indian officials.

Raman was also kept busy monitoring developments off the field. Early in the tour notice was given of a court case to be brought by the Civil Rights Vigilance Group of Bangalore seeking to have the visas of Boycott and Cook revoked. A petition signed by 54 law professors, students and jurists claimed that the Gleneagles agreement had been breached. Fortunately for the cricketers the case was thrown out, but as the team moved to Calcutta, fresh protests arose around the team's hotel with a New Year's Eve gathering giving the police a chance to wield their lathi sticks against some 200 placard-bearing students.

Amid the rich tapestry of experience that will always be India a degree of adversity can help bring a team together. Spartan conditions have long characterised tours of India, though Raman acknowledges a pleasant surprise at how much hotel and restaurant facilities had improved in the more remote locations since his visit with the Commonwealth side, with English cuisine generally available for those who didn't care for an endless diet of curry. The food in prospect had even been sufficiently unthreatening to persuade Geoff Boycott that he could risk a visit to a country he had previously chosen not to tour. He was nevertheless in for a bit of a shock. Perhaps his standards were more demanding than those of others. Writing of the boredom of touring, he looked forward to his evening meals as a relief from the tedium but then found much of the food 'when identifiable, was monotonous and tasteless'. Other creature comforts were in short supply. Beds in Nagpur had been only 5 foot 3 inches long; in Jammu they had been damp. Hunting parties had set off after rats and snakes and the key to catching cockroaches was 'to leave the light off until you are ready, then flick it on and whack them before they have time to run for cover.'

Whatever the off-field tribulations, Boycott had travelled to India with a personal mission: the record aggregate of runs for all Test cricket, held by Garry Sobers, lay within his sights. At Delhi he had achieved his target. Yet he had done so at a pace that had not helped England's chances of moving to a position from which they could press for victory. Remarks from the captain that he was hoping for runs to be scored more quickly reached Boycott's ears when the headlines of press comment in England were relayed to him. Always enjoying a story with Boycott at its centre, some journalists had no doubt exaggerated such criticism as Fletcher may have made of the batting of his two century-makers, Tavaré also having earned some adverse publicity for the pace of his 149, albeit his runs came quicker than Boycott's.

Raman was required to mend bridges between the captain and his opening batsman with the dispute hinging on the extent to which Fletcher's words had been critical and whether or not he had told his batsmen to get a move on during the Delhi match. Fletcher issued an apology, though whether it was ever seriously required remained a matter for debate, the *Times* correspondent's sympathies lying entirely with the captain. Whatever the rights and wrongs, it was an unhappy appetiser for what lay round the corner with Boycott.

At Calcutta Boycott played his final Test for England. He did so complaining that he had not felt well. His problems had begun in Delhi, where he had awoken with a temperature and diarrhoea. He had seen a doctor at the British High Commission, who had diagnosed a viral infection. Raman had suggested that he remain in Delhi then follow the main party to Calcutta. Despite all, he had travelled to Calcutta and gone into the Test match feeling weak. His two innings brought him scores of 18 and 6. Out in his second innings on the third evening, he took no further part in the match. His dismissal came immediately ahead of the rest day, after which a substitute took the field on his behalf. Advised by Bernie Thomas, the team physiotherapist, to take some fresh air, on the final day of the match he ventured to the ground, where he needed to sort out his kit. There he enquired of Geoff Cook and Paul Allott, who were not in the Test team, whether they would care to accompany him for a few holes of golf. Finding no response to his offer, Boycott then set off for the Tollygunj Club in the elite suburbs of Calcutta, where among those surprised to see him was Anne Subba Row, who had flown out to join Raman. Boycott had not intended that there should be any secret about his game of golf, but he had left the cricket ground without seeking permission from the captain or manager. It was seen as inappropriate behaviour for any member of the touring party, and for his colleagues it confirmed their feeling that he was a poor team player.

That evening Boycott was summoned to see Raman, with Fletcher, vice-captain Willis and Thomas, in his role as assistant manager, in attendance. Knowing that the rest of the team were incensed at his behaviour, they demanded that Boycott apologise to them. A short note to this effect was stuck to the fridge door, where the team's beers were stored, while the management team deliberated over what to do with their most prolific run-maker. Their unanimous decision was that Boycott should return home. Seeking authority on the matter from TCCB, they received the reply that the decision was theirs to take. Initially Boycott appeared relieved to be returning to England, but when independent medical examinations found nothing wrong with him, he announced that he was prepared to stay on. It was a response which found no favour with Raman and his management team. With the rest of the touring party having departed for their zonal match at Jamshedpur, Raman escorted Boycott to the airport, delaying until after his departure an official statement that he had left the tour. The explanation offered was that 'physical problems had affected his mental approach.'

'I didn't send him home,' Raman says years later. 'I had every reason to do so, but I didn't.' With Boycott, unlike the rest of the team, Raman did not enjoy a good reputation. The Yorkshireman found his manager suffered from 'excessive diplomacy', too quickly giving in to all the demands of the Indian Board. 'Pure bloody-mindedness' was Boycott's pithy verdict on his manager's refusal to allow him to return to Delhi to see the one doctor who had diagnosed problems with his health. 'I reckon he was glad to see the back of me,' he wrote, 'and the feeling was mutual.'

A tour that had kept the players away from home for more than three arduous months ended with further matches in Sri Lanka. Two close 45-over games were shared, England taking the first by five runs and the hosts squeezing home by three runs in the second. A well-fought Test match was won by England by seven wickets, principally thanks to the bowling of Underwood in the first innings and Emburey in the second.

As he looks back on a difficult tour, Raman reflects happily on his return to the land of his paternal roots, of which he and Anne have grown so fond. 'Originally when the British left they said, "Thank God they've gone. At last we've got our own country." Then after a very short time they had changed completely. They were saying, "Thank Goodness they came and started this all off." Otherwise where would we be? They are very pro-British, in my view.'

Cricket matches on the Maidan in Mumbai, 2016

19

'You weren't always sure what he was up to'

Chairman of TCCB

While Raman's energies in the early 1980s had been primarily directed towards the welfare of Surrey, from 1 October 1985 the focus of his attention was once again the national scene. On this date he replaced Charles Palmer as chairman of TCCB. His name had earlier been proposed when George Mann was elected in 1978 and again when Palmer took over in 1983. Raman was not keen on entering a third contest, but he found himself unopposed. At a time when the dividing lines between MCC and TCCB were both confusing and increasingly contentious, he could be seen as less of an establishment figure than his two predecessors, Palmer having already been president of MCC while Mann's presidential term began just twelve months after relinquishing office at TCCB. Of those with a foot in both camps, none has more clearly worn the TCCB shirt than Raman, and this is how it would remain.

Raman was to find himself embroiled in challenges on all fronts throughout the five years he held office. For the England team there was to be a string of on-field disappointments, with scandal on and off the field to spice the dish for the media. But before the worst of these problems erupted, Raman was engaged in battles closer to home. With the passage of time and with more money flowing into the game, the relationship between TCCB and MCC had become more fractious. George Mann, as president of MCC, had come with unusually close ties to TCCB and his chosen successor, Jack Davies also embraced some sympathy for TCCB's increasing demands to be able to run cricket – and cricket at Lord's – as they saw fit. The main stumbling block to peaceful negotiation was MCC secretary Jack Bailey. A man with whom Raman had worked harmoniously and constructively in their younger days, Bailey was now hell-bent on safeguarding the rights of his members. 'He was very protective as far as MCC was concerned. Well that was his job,' Raman now concedes. In Ossie Wheatley's eyes Bailey would have flourished in the Brexit debate. 'He could only ever see one side of the story.'

Behind the TCCB's endeavours was the financial welfare of the whole game. The counties were heavily reliant on their hand-out from the centre, typically some 40% of their total income, and within TCCB there was inevitable conflict between those counties who staged Test matches and the rest. To the extent that the Test ground counties made more money, they argued that they had vastly greater year-round expenses; but within TCCB they were outnumbered by the smaller counties.

MCC presented different problems again, and there was a new complexion to their situation when a formula was agreed whereby the Test ground counties were permitted to retain the advertising revenue at their grounds while foregoing much of the money coming in from other sources. The whole concept of being told what to do when matches were held on his ground never went down well with Bailey, and Derek Newton remembers being with Raman to talk about a TCCB requirement that there should be full perimeter advertising. It was a request that did not suit MCC whose preference had been to forego income from advertising in favour of allowing spectators onto the grass. 'This was the final straw for Jack Bailey. Raman said, "Jack, Lord's will lose Test matches if you don't go along with it."'

To lose a Test match would have been unthinkable for MCC, for whom the main attraction to most members is their ability to sit in the pavilion for the traditional mid-summer Test. A symbiotic, if uneasy, relationship has always existed between MCC and TCCB/ECB. Lord's is the ground where tickets sell most readily despite costing more than elsewhere. Moreover, to play in a Test at Lord's is the dream of every overseas cricketer. So in reality TCCB has always needed MCC as much as the other way round. Only since the growth in the number of Test grounds has the risk of being deprived of a second Test in the same summer become a threat with meaning for MCC.

Early in his year of presidency Jack Davies acceded to a request for a joint MCC/TCCB liaison committee to be set up to consider the running of major matches at Lord's. For Bailey it was, to quote the relevant chapter heading in his book, 'the beginning of the end'. There were endless arguments when the liaison committee met with bitter wrangling over the detail of the subsequent minutes. A catalyst for further disharmony was the approaching celebration of MCC's two hundredth anniversary. It was to be marked by a match between MCC and the Rest of the World, a showpiece game for which the club had negotiated the availability of most of the world's leading stars. The fixture impacted upon TCCB in the sense that it rendered impractical the holding of a sixth Test that summer. For this TCCB were to be compensated by MCC. Bailey's book contains details of protracted arguments culminating in the amount of compensation reasonably due. Bailey's calculations made two inaccurate assumptions: that the lost match would have been against Pakistan and that extra money would have been forthcoming for it from the sponsor. He was later to discover that England's theoretical opponents would have been Sri Lanka and that sponsorship money was for the season not on a match by match basis. Bailey's proffered figure, at £260,000, was therefore about twice what he might otherwise have suggested.

By the time Bailey was wanting to retract his suggested figure, it had been broadcast to others within TCCB as the expected contribution from MCC. Two obstinate men opposed each other across the table when Raman met with Bailey in the coming weeks, and MCC's secretary was finding less support than he felt he had a right to expect from his own side. He believed that he was giving away more of MCC members' money than was right, and he had had to give ground on other matters such as TCCB's insistence on making payment by credit card available – Raman moving with or ahead of the tide as usual, whereas for Bailey it meant administrative costs and sacrificing 2.6% on the price of each ticket bought in this way. When Bailey found himself without the support he had once expected from Davies's successor Colin Cowdrey, resignation soon became his only option. No previous secretary had departed MCC in this manner. Raman had been billed as the principal adversary in the whole unhappy saga. He, in turn, had served the cause of cricket as he saw it, and it was a sad ending to what had once been a fruitful partnership at the heart of commercial thinking at Lord's.

Was it just a clash of personalities? Others such as Peter Lush have said Bailey was a difficult man with whom to deal, but Raman's firmness had put down important markers for the future. Dealings with Bailey's successor, John Stephenson, certainly proved easier, 'especially with David Clark out of the way too,' Bernie Coleman comments. However, after Raman and Coleman had both moved on, Roger Knight, who was installed as Secretary of MCC in 1994, later acquiring the title chief executive, inherited a situation that he found far from easy. 'It was difficult because there was a percentage of ticket income due to TCCB and a much smaller percentage to MCC. Advertising, hospitality and the food and drink outlets paid MCC, but nothing had been agreed in writing. There had been an assumption over the years that TCCB would dictate and that ECB would continue to do the same.'

If Knight was more fortunate than Bailey in the support forthcoming from his committee, he still had to face threats from Lord MacLaurin that Test cricket might be taken away from Lord's, and there was some unpleasantness before Staging Agreements were in place. As the number of Test grounds has risen to nine in the current millennium with too few matches to satisfy them, Knight comments that bidding processes have taken some counties to the verge of bankruptcy. Yet ECB is awash with funds. What was once the baby that Raman nurtured towards maturity has become a giant, and one that many now feel may have too much power for its own good.

Raman was soon making changes to ensure more effective governance of English cricket. At TCCB he inherited a business that by the end of his term would be turning over some £25 million, about five times the figure just ten years earlier. He felt that such an enterprise required a more streamlined structure, something akin to the way a typical trading company might operate. The full board on which all the counties were represented met three times a year and was an inevitably cumbersome body for decision making. 'I was dealing with a game demanding action much more quickly than in the past. You couldn't just wait for committees to assemble before you could take action,' he explains. So Raman determined that the smaller executive committee, involving all the heads of department and meeting at least monthly, should be given more teeth. Part of the new structure was upgrading the role of the secretary, and when Alan Smith moved from Warwickshire to take over from Donald Carr in 1986 it was as chief executive.

Smith soon learned to respect his chairman. 'He was highly intelligent, and a brilliant memo and letter writer. There were no wasted words in a Subba Row letter or memo; and he was skilled in dealing with the media. And Raman was always full of ideas, many very good, some less so, but he didn't enjoy it if one of his ideas was pushed down!' Like many ideas men, Raman was not always the easiest to work with and Smith became used to the telephone ringing late in the evening 'but that was the way he was when he got an idea, and if it was an unusual hour, so be it.' He could also sense the frustration when Raman found himself questioned by his more conservative colleagues who had grown used to the protracted business of bringing everything to committee. A clash of styles almost inevitably goes with a mover and shaker, as Raman undoubtedly was.

The years of Raman's chairmanship coincided with ever-growing problems with the broadcasting contracts. It was Bernie Coleman and Peter Lush who bore the brunt of the troubled negotiations. Coleman had a long track record of successful dealings with the media going back to 1972 when he had enabled cricket pictures to gain their rightful place on the back pages of the national newspapers. Until that time only one box camera behind the bowler's arm had been permitted at Test matches. Coleman remembers that half the sports editors based in London had never been to Lord's. He soon rectified this, arranging a visit and asking what was needed to improve pictorial coverage. 'If only we could get our cameramen into the ground,' they said. The initial response from the Board exuded establishment reservations. 'We can't have cameramen running all over the place,' Coleman remembers being told. 'I said, "Gentlemen, if you want coverage, this is what we must do." It was the first year Patrick Eagar got into Lord's ground.'

In the late 1970s, with ITV having ceased to show any interest in cricket, 'a scandal' in Coleman's view, there was still only the BBC in a position to bid for television rights and they believed themselves to have a monopoly on radio broadcasting, only to find Coleman and Lush prepared to float the idea of a network of commercial radio channels taking up the chance instead. While the BBC spoke of moral blackmail and depriving blind people of the chance to follow the game, Coleman battled on for what he regarded as a fair fee for a summer's Tests.

By the late 1980s change was on the horizon. Satellite and cable television were now in the offing, though the number of viewers they could offer to advertisers was still small. Raman was, however, one of the first to see the new opportunities and was personally involved in the setting up of Croydon Cable television in his home area and in opening the operators' eyes to the possibilities that lay within sport. 'Well before BSB and Sky because he had the vision to see what was going to happen,' says Bernie Coleman. The notion of people paying for what they might wish to watch was dear to Coleman's heart. 'Let us have a channel where the people have the opportunity to buy the best,' he said in a press interview, envisaging not just Test match cricket but Luciano Pavarotti at Covent Garden becoming available to those prepared to pay, while advertisers would be subsidising the costs involved.

In July 1987, as chairman of TCCB, Raman used the correspondence columns of *The Times* to endorse these views. Bemoaning the government's meagre support through the Sports Council, he went on: 'What needs to happen is a denationalisation of our televised sport here in the UK. As long as sport is tied either to the BBC, whose funds are inevitably restricted by the licence fee, or to ITV, whose interests are principally motivated by their shareholders, it will not secure a proper share of the revenue it both deserves and needs.'

'There is an answer,' his letter continued. 'The technology of satellite, cable and microwave services is advancing at such a pace that before long we are going to be able to add any number of new channels to the existing system. Furthermore, the user of these services can be required to pay for what he or she wants – in the same way as we pay for our gas, electricity and telephone.' As we sit back and watch our cricket on Sky, it may be difficult to acknowledge how far-thinking Raman and Coleman were 30 years ago.

With the emergence of BSB and Sky the prospect of competition at last became a feature of the televising of sport. However, the early merger of the two companies became a cause of concern and by late 1990 Coleman was pleading for advertising or pay-to-view services coming to the BBC.

'Exhibiting great endurance through all kinds of trials, annoyances, or provocations' is Wikipedia's definition of 'the patience of Job.' Sifting through a mountain of paperwork that Bernie Coleman has preserved, the biblical analogy is never far from the mind. A full reconstruction of all that went on through the meetings and correspondence that engulfed Coleman and Lush in 1989 may be a fruitful subject for a researcher not primarily concerned with the life of Raman.

There were no holds barred as Coleman and Lush strove to bring into cricket the money the game desperately needed through striking a better deal with the BBC. Marmaduke Hussey, at the time the Corporation's chairman, was approached on a personal level by Brian Downing, another from the marketing team at the Oval with strong media experience, but to no avail. Coleman forged links with Mark McCormack's International Management Group. Home secretaries Willie Whitelaw and Douglas Hurd were bombarded with correspondence, as was the Cabinet Office. Always there was the fear that, as the new satellite stations sought to build their customer base through syphoning off the most popular sporting events, so the rights of terrestrial stations would continue to be protected by a government anxious to be seen as the friend of the man in the street, the voter, who had long grown used to watching the FA Cup Final and the Grand National as of right through paying his licence fee. Of course a case could as readily be made for Test cricket. Without easy access to seeing their heroes in action, where would the next Ian Botham come from?

If Coleman and Lush were in the front line, their Board chairman was never far away, as Lush well remembers, if not wholly positively. 'Raman used to go off and do his own thing without telling anybody. With the BBC, he'd tell you after he'd seen them.' Yes, there is an impulsive streak in Raman. His good ideas cannot always be restrained – he must act! 'It could undermine what you were doing,' Lush explains. 'You weren't always sure what he was up to.'

In October 1989 came a press release that provided the first evidence that the years of lobbying had not been in vain: 'In a British broadcasting first, Sky Television is to transmit coverage of the entire England cricket tour of the West Indies LIVE.' The new world was opening up. For the privileged few with their satellite dishes in place, winter evenings would be spent watching live cricket, thanks to Sky and the West Indies Cricket Board. Fuller fruits of the lobbying of Raman and his colleagues lay years ahead. By 1998, with Brian Downing behind the marketing effort and Lord MacLaurin bringing political clout to the chairmanship at the newly formed ECB, Channel Four broke the BBC monopoly for home Tests, with Sky taking over in 2006,

148

bringing steadily enhanced quality to the transmission of international cricket and swelling the central coffers to the overall benefit of the game.

Taking over as chairman in 1985, Raman had been instrumental in forming an international committee, while a revolutionary change was the creation of the new job of England team manager, a post to which Micky Stewart was the first appointment. Stewart had long believed that the England team required someone to fill just such a role, and he brought relevant experience from his time with Surrey. But he took over a team in some disarray. In 1985 David Gower had enjoyed a splendid summer leading England to a 3 – 1 win against Australia, but the side he took to the West Indies was soundly beaten by the world's strongest team. With all five Tests lost by a wide margin, a merry social life and a lackadaisical attitude to practice fuelled the case for those who questioned Gower's right to retain the captaincy. He was allowed just one more Test in the following summer before a five wicket defeat by India saw Mike Gatting installed in his stead. India went on to win a three-Test series 2 – 0, and when New Zealand sealed an eight-wicket victory at Trent Bridge, it was enough to give the summer's second visitors their first series win on English soil.

That winter saw Peter Lush forsake his desk at Lord's to take on the management of the tour to Australia. With Stewart in his new role and a captain who shared his attitude to hard work, the critics were defied and, despite some lacklustre performances in the early matches, the Ashes were retained. In the ensuing summer a series of five Tests was played against Pakistan. England had their moments, but the weather took care of the first two matches, Pakistan won handsomely at Headingley, England fell just short in an 18-over run chase at Edgbaston and lost the series at the Oval, salvaging a draw from a match in which the visitors had made 708 in their first innings. Some of the national team's weaknesses were plain to see.

That winter England came as close as they have ever done to winning the World Cup, losing by seven runs to Australia in the final at Calcutta. The tournament had taken the players around both India and Pakistan. As soon as it was over, they began a tour of Pakistan. Coming so soon after a contentious series in England, it was not enlightened planning by the ICC, and it would lead to traumas that would test even Raman's powers of diplomacy.

20

'The umpires are not going to stand tomorrow'

Sorting out problems in Pakistan

Of the many challenges Raman faced as chairman of TCCB none can have matched those flowing from the incident made memorable by the photograph of England captain Mike Gatting angrily prodding his finger at Pakistani umpire Shakoor Rana. Taken late on the second day of the Test match at Faisalabad, it is a picture available to the world's press only because, while others had shut up shop for the night, English photographer Graham Morris alone had remained to capture the image. The main facts behind the story it told are simply related. England, one down in the three-match series, were on top in the game and pressing for another over before the close. Wishing to stop a single being taken, Gatting summoned his long leg, David Capel, to come in closer. As the bowler, Eddie Hemmings, began to run in, Gatting signalled to indicate that Capel had come far enough. This action was deemed unfair by Shakoor Rana, standing at square leg, who called dead ball, an action that annoyed Gatting, not least because it rendered less probable the chance of another over. An altercation followed between captain and umpire, though what was being said was not apparent from off the field.

The team returned to their hotel unaware of the severity of the looming problem. In the words of manager Peter Lush, 'I remember very vividly getting a call in my room from a member of the press saying "Do you realise that the umpires are not going to stand tomorrow?" It shook me. I didn't know that.' Next day, to the surprise of most of the England party, the umpires did indeed refuse to take the field and made clear that they would not do so until a formal apology had been received from the England captain. Gatting, maintaining he had done nothing wrong, refused to comply and an impasse ensued with no play that day. Nor was the matter resolved to allow a resumption on the rest day that followed. Eventually, with a day's play lost, a scrappy two line note was reluctantly written and signed by Gatting. Play then resumed, but too much time had been lost and, with further deductions for questionable light, the match petered out as a draw.

Behind the bare facts lay important background factors, but the headlines alone were enough for pontification from those close to the action and the larger number passing comment from afar. For many of the latter, those involved in the upper echelons of running the English domestic game and those sounding

Mike Gatting and Shakoor Rana

off in the correspondence columns of the newspapers, an England captain had behaved disgracefully and should be stripped of office. Those closer to the scene of the crime had rather different perspectives. Robin Marlar, in Pakistan for *The Sunday Times*, is one whose sympathies are firmly with the England team. At pains to stress the history of playing cricket against Pakistan, he speaks fondly of many of the country's early stars – 'Fazal Mahmood, he was a real gent' – and he recounts how the Eaglets, many of them future Test players, as part of their tours to England had the values of the game drilled into them by Alf Gover. But more latterly he had seen standards drop and he knew political interference was rife. The situation had not been improved by TCCB's refusal the previous summer to back down when there had been objections to David Constant standing as umpire in the Tests, despite the Pakistan management's insistence that he had made crucial errors against their team on their previous tour. Now, in Pakistan, TCCB's intransigence was to become a wild card in the pack for local officialdom, a way of evening up the score.

Marlar had seen with his own eyes truly atrocious umpiring in the previous Test at Lahore. Abdul Qadir's leg spinners may have been too good for England's batsmen, but coach Micky Stewart, in private correspondence to his wife now in the public domain, has written that nine of the England wickets were 'umpired out'. For Marlar a more accurate figure is 12 or 13. And he goes on: 'You cannot play cricket in those circumstances, I don't care who you are. And all those people who say it's only a game have no understanding of what it means to have cricket as your profession.' Emphasising his point, Marlar's voice rises: 'That team at Lahore was put through an experience which frankly must never ever happen again.' In case there is any doubt how passionately he means what he is saying, he repeats this last sentence.

So the umpiring was poor, the officials, notably Shakeel Khan, incompetent. Had there been DRS at the time, Peter Lush believes there would have been many different outcomes. 'It got to people,' he says, 'because they felt they weren't getting a fair crack of the whip. When you are playing for your career, you expect everything to be fair and reasonable. And when you are beaten hollow, as we were in the first Test, it pierces the heart' But was the umpiring biased? 'Well who knows?' Lush replies, reluctant to commit further. By contrast, Micky Stewart has reported evidence passed from two former Pakistan players that the umpires were fixed, while Robin Marlar is in emphatic mode again, his measured tones abandoned as he almost bellows: 'I have absolutely no doubt whatsoever.' Marlar's contention is consistent with statistics furnished by Scyld Berry. 'By the time of the Karachi Test,' he has written, '101 Pakistani batsmen had been given leg-before-wicket by their own umpires in home Tests, against 196 visiting batsmen.'

It was known that, before the Test matches began, the Pakistan players had been summoned to receive a message from their country's president General Zia-ul-Haq himself. The national side had just succumbed 3 – 0 in the one-day matches and, with an election looming, General Zia could not afford to lose the Test series as well. The players delivered an emphatic victory for the general at Lahore; but if the umpires were also mindful of a national duty, they too had performed with flying colours. Cricket has had its tempestuous tours with Bodyline the most widely cited and it has had its match-fixing scandals, but have the values of the game ever been so degraded as in this morale-sapping series in Pakistan? Robin Marlar thinks not. 'It's worse than the players cheating – to have the umpires cheating by state control.'

Cheating. That is a nasty allegation in any sport. Yet the actual word, heard on the field by Nick Cook among others, was directed at the England captain by umpire Shakoor Rana. Cook remembers the whole incident well. He was fielding at midwicket and hoping to bowl the final over at the new batsman. This was why Capel had been brought in for the fifth ball – to keep Salim Malik off strike and let Cook bowl at his partner, Aamer Malik, who had just come to the crease in his first Test match. 'Salim knew what was happening,' Cook says. Technically Gatting's final signal to Capel might just have been construed as having infringed the Laws, though they were less specific on fielder movement than they have since become, but Salim Malik later acknowledged that he had been told that an adjustment was being made.

'He swore at Gatt,' says Nick Cook. 'Shakoor Rana called him a f*****g cheat.' And therein lay the nub of why the on-field fracas blew up into an incident of international proportions. Because no-one is happy to be labelled a cheat. There had been no intention to cheat, but to those who knew Shakoor, his behaviour typified an umpire whose self-important interference had already manifested itself as an irritant to the players. For Mike Gatting the accusation that he was a cheat meant that it was Shakoor who needed to do the apologising. And in the stance he took his team were solidly behind him: there would be no one-sided apology.

With his side benefitting from any delay, the contribution of Pakistan captain Javed Miandad in strengthening Shakoor's resolve not to apologise was unhelpful, while the team manager, Haseeb Ahsan, still perhaps smarting from English umpires questioning his bowling action when he had toured as an off spinner in 1962, was also uncooperative, making plain to anyone who was interested his utter disdain for Gatting.

Meanwhile back in England the lines between Lord's and Pakistan were buzzing, and one causing the BT bill to soar at the TCCB was Raman.

Attitudes at home were influenced by an earlier disciplinary incident in Pakistan. Lush and his management team were thought to have taken too soft a line in the first Test in dealing with Chris Broad when he had lingered an age at the wicket after being given out in the second innings. For this he had received only a reprimand. Now, following the finger pointing by the England captain, Ted Dexter led the public call for stern action, while Colin Moynihan, the Minister of Sport, told the House of Commons that 'flouting of the authority of umpires and referees cannot be excused in any circumstances.' Others were quicker to defend Gatting. 'If the umpire had told me I was a cheat, I might have said a few things back. It is ridiculous for such an incompetent umpire to accuse Gatting of that,' said Ray Illingworth. Tom Graveney was even more forthright: 'They have been cheating us for 37 years and I think the tour should be called off immediately.'

Raman was not short of advice, measured or otherwise. With chief executive Alan Smith closely involved, once it was known that play had not been resumed, he leapt to action. Calls were put through to the president of the Pakistan Board, General Safdar Butt, following which Peter Lush was led to believe that the matter had been sorted out. This was to prove far from the truth. Raman recalls his impression of what was going to happen after his calls to the general. 'I understood "sorting it out" to mean that there would be an all-round shaking of hands and that would be the end of it. But then the general did nothing.'

Back in Faisalabad the secretary to the Pakistan Board had chosen to leave the ground without the courtesy of telling the England party. Still seeing no evidence of the action Raman had assured him would happen, Peter Lush set off for Lahore to seek out the president of the Board in person. The general had an engagement that evening, and it was not until the following morning that a meeting was possible. When Lush arrived, he found a representative of the press sitting alongside the president. The meeting produced no magic formula for re-starting the match. With the impasse still unresolved, the TCCB instruction was to get the players back on the field at all costs. John Woodcock, on the spot for *The Times*, was one who felt the England management should have taken a firmer hand in getting the captain to climb down. To Peter Lush it was not that simple. He knew he had an obstinate captain, and he acknowledges that 'the job of a captain is to be above it all.' But he goes on: 'You can only recommend to people what you think they should do. You cannot ultimately tell them.' Lush was not prepared to force his captain to the point of resignation. Ultimately Gatting signed his two-liner only because he feared for the future of younger players on the fringe of the row and because Graham Gooch suggested that a parallel statement be issued deploring the pressure put upon the players by their employer. This statement, flying in the face of the players' contracts, was duly issued and play resumed in the Test match.

Meanwhile in London, as chance would have it, one of the TCCB's three full board meetings held each year had been scheduled for Thursday, 10 December, the rest day in the Test. Delegates had met for dinner the night before and that afternoon there had been a meeting of the smaller executive committee, with Raman as chairman at the centre of affairs. The problems in Faisalabad had been the main topic over the dinner, but the whole matter only arose in 'other business' at the Board's meeting next day. When such topics as the experimental uncovering of pitches and residential requirements for overseas players had been exhausted, only 40 minutes remained for the burning issue of the troubles in Pakistan. Raman was able to reassure all of the efforts he and Smith had been making to get the match re-started, and it was agreed that a full enquiry would be held once the players had returned. The priority was to ensure that the tour continued. This was certainly the wish of the Foreign Office, while an early return could have led to fresh arguments between the two boards about the financial consequences.

It was as peacemakers that Raman and Smith presented themselves to the media. 'Every effort must be made to restart the match tomorrow morning' was the keynote line in the official statement. Meanwhile the text of the players' statement that accompanied Gatting's apology made clear the players' hostility to the Board back in England. After deploring that it had not been possible to effect a compromise solution and making plain that Shakoor Rana had used 'foul and abusive' language, the players added: 'We also wish to register a unanimous protest that the TCCB should consider it necessary to issue instructions through our manager, Peter Lush, to order the captain to make an unconditional apology to the umpire.'

The players' statement was published in the English press on the Saturday, the final day of the ill-fated Test in Faisalabad. By this time it was known that Raman and Alan Smith would be flying out to Karachi, the venue for the final Test, which was due to start on the Wednesday. Both had experience of managing teams on the sub-continent, Smith having taken England on a difficult tour of Pakistan four years earlier. 'It's never been an easy place to tour,' he says, recalling the variable standards of the hotels with the only chance of a drink dependent on the High Commission's generosity. Raman and Smith departed on the Sunday evening, reassuring the press that the England captain was not about to be sacked. They knew that a hostile reception awaited them, with Gatting reported as saying he was not inclined to play in the next Test until he had sorted out one or two matters with the

TCCB hierarchy. If he had cared to read the local papers, Gatting's mood might have lifted at this juncture. *The Nation*, published in Lahore, carried an article by Nasir Abbas Mirza, a friend of Imran Khan, citing Haseeb Ahsan and Javed Miandad as 'a perfect example of the maxim that give a small man power and he will show you how small he is.' Mirza's article went on to suggest that the aim of the Pakistan establishment was 'not only to win at all costs but to frustrate the opposition by blatant cheating.'

Missing no opportunity to stir the troubles, and justifying the comments in *The Nation*, the Pakistan authorities chose the time of Raman's arrival to announce the umpires for the third Test. Shakeel Khan, whose decision making at Lahore had first lit the touch paper for the series, was to stand with Khizer Hayat, Shakoor's comparatively innocent partner at Faisalabad. Eventually Shakeel was replaced by Mahboob Shah, generally regarded as Pakistan's best umpire, with whom Khizer Hayat had stood and given general satisfaction in the World Cup. But this decision was made only after the suggestion of umpires coming from India had proved impractical, while Haseeb had histrionically taken the chance to volunteer that he would personally pay for Bird and Shepherd to be flown in from England – or even Constant! It all served to give Raman a better idea of life at the coalface.

A strong man he has often shown himself to be, but Raman remains a diplomat at heart. Never was his natural charm more needed than when he prepared to face his initial meeting with the players. On arrival Raman and Smith spoke first to the press. Then, before seeing the team, Raman sought advice from his friend Robin Marlar, who emphasised to him the depth of feelings in the camp. If the players had expected a rough ride, they were pleased to find that Raman's tone was one of conciliation. He had set out on a fact-finding mission; he had not come as an old-fashioned schoolmaster cane in hand. 'I don't think we fully realised the players' frustration, just as the players were probably unaware of how very strong the Board's views are on dissent,' he said after the meeting. For John Woodcock Raman was perhaps a little too conciliatory. 'It is important that Subba Row should not be persuaded that the faults are all on one side,' he commented.

Mike Gatting had been chosen to captain England because he brought something of the bulldog determination to the task. These were the qualities that enabled his partnership with Micky Stewart to flourish. His reputation had always been as a man who played the game fairly, but had the need for diplomacy headed the list of requirements for the job in Pakistan, his name would not have topped the list. He was prepared to admit inappropriate on-field behaviour, but he still looked for an apology and Raman's mission was to extract one. He recalls an early meeting with General Butt. 'I told him he couldn't say he was going to sort something out and then do absolutely nothing. He said, "It's very difficult in my country." I said, "It's bloody difficult in mine. I don't care about yours."' They were to meet on six occasions before Raman's departure, even dining together quite amicably; but with no apology forthcoming, the underlying row did not abate. Then when General Butt unexpectedly indicated that Shakoor Rana might be persuaded to apologise, he found Raman with appropriate text already drafted and ready for signature.

The note read: 'Having thought about the Faisalabad match and your gracious apology, I feel the future of cricketing relations between Pakistan and England would be helped if I too expressed my regrets over the incident. I hope you will accept this apology in the spirit in which it is given.' The note was duly taken away with the promise that it would be returned to Raman before he had to leave his hotel. Predictably there was a delay in tracking down Shakoor Rana. Eventually, just before Raman was due to depart for the airport, the signed note returned in the hands of Ijaz Butt, the Board secretary. There were just two problems. The first was that there had been one small change to the text: in the signed version the word 'apology' was missing from the second sentence. The second problem for Raman was that Gatting was not around at the hotel.

This was to present further difficulties for Peter Lush, whose job it was to release the statement to the press, once he had shown the amended text to Gatting. 'The note was altered in such a way that Mike Gatting refused to accept it,' Lush explains. 'Therefore I didn't release it. This upset Raman very much. But the Pakistan Board had altered it – there was a different meaning to it.' The crucial change was made clear to those concerned when TCCB's enquiry into the whole unhappy business was held in early January, allowing Gatting to explain to those present why the note had been unacceptable to him. Nevertheless, Lush now feels that his failure to release the statement in Pakistan impaired his longer-term relationship with Raman. Viewing the whole saga nearly 30 years later, Raman expresses surprise that the statement with or without the critical word should not have been regarded as sufficiently apologetic in tone to satisfy Gatting. 'The whole thing is an apology. The word "apology", as far as I am concerned, doesn't matter.'

Before his return to England, Raman took upon himself a decision that would have far-reaching effects. Having seen the hardships the players had suffered at first hand, he decreed that they should all receive a special bonus of £1,000 in addition to their tour fee of £5,000. It was a controversial decision and one for which he had not sought authority from his colleagues on the TCCB executive committee. Alan Smith remembers Raman mentioning the idea of the £1,000. He had not felt strongly about the wisdom of this very unusual course of action, but he had imagined that it was a matter for discussion back in England.

In making his gesture at the end of his visit, Raman passed on to the tour manager the responsibility for telling the players. Peter Lush was unsure how the players would feel, but he was not happy about the idea. 'Raman said, "It's your job to tell them." I felt that if that was what he wanted to do, it was more appropriate if he told them. He said, "I'm going back to England tomorrow anyway; it's now in your hands." So I was instructed to tell the players and that is what I did. And one or two of them thought they were being bought off. So they didn't decline the payment, but they didn't like it. Neil Foster, in particular, said it was wrong. And I thought it was wrong.' Lush's view was shared by Micky Stewart, and subsequent press reports indicate that the influential Graham Gooch was another disenchanted by the gesture. 'It was a nice thought,' says Nick Cook, 'but misguided, because as soon as it appeared in the press whatever sympathy there was for the players evaporated.'

The match, in which England had at one stage seemed well placed, moved in favour of Pakistan on the fourth day with umpiring decisions returning to the headlines as the first three England batsmen to be dismissed lingered unduly long at the crease, expressions of surprise boiling over to off-field dissent by the England captain, now close to the end of his tether. Commentators have suggested that the umpiring in the match was of a generally acceptable standard, but suspicions were fuelled by what had gone on earlier. On the final day a determined rearguard innings by Emburey secured a draw for England.

By this time news of the payment, intended to be confidential, had reached the press, as it inevitably would at some stage. Back in England, Alan Smith was defending Raman's actions in making the special award: 'We have made it as a vote of confidence in the players and a way of thanking them for the way they have picked themselves up after their recent problems.' To Peter Lush the payment had always been Raman's idea, but Robin Marlar now reveals the part he played. He recalls how, when Raman had first consulted him in Karachi, he had warned him that the players were in imminent danger of going home – they had actually voted to do so, though Micky Stewart and others managed to persuade them against doing so. Marlar had added his own view: 'They are entitled to go home because they shouldn't be asked to play when the thing is rigged.' Stressing to Raman that he had to do something on the spot, Marlar was mindful of advice given to him by one of cricket's most enduring administrators. 'He taught me over the years that the

Raman in Pakistan

only way to motivate the professional cricketer is through the pocket. It's not the way I think. I don't like to treat people as if they are bloody mercenaries, but if that's the way it's got to be, that's the way it's got to be.' To Marlar the notion of £1,000 was 'proportional', not too small a sum and not too large. And the urgency of the situation, as Marlar saw it, meant that there was no time to defer to London. So the seed was sown in Raman's mind, though he only turned Marlar's advice into action days later when his attempts to squeeze an apology out of the offending umpire and his board appeared to have failed.

Back in England Raman faced criticism on two counts: the action he had taken was considered ill-conceived and it had been taken without due authority. Some members of the executive committee felt that a matter of principle had been at stake, and Alan Smith believes that it didn't help that they first heard of the payment when they read about it in the press. Derek Newton, speaking from the vantage point of one who has been chairman of a FTSE company and as one who knows Raman well, believes that he was within his rights to act as he did. 'If you've got a chairman and a chief executive who decide on a matter of some urgency that a certain action has

159

got to be taken, then you can hardly say one of them is going out on a limb if they both agreed.' Newton here assumes some more positive endorsement of the action by Alan Smith than appears to have been the case. He goes on to say that he was surprised by the course of action taken, but he recalls Raman's words when he came back: 'You weren't there. With the atmosphere out there, something had to be done.'

Robin Marlar, for one, remains adamant that Raman deserved fuller backing from his board than he was subsequently to receive. Moreover, recent enquiries have established that there were those who had initially voiced support who were later to desert Raman when the adverse publicity built up. In Marlar's judgement Raman was shabbily treated and his long-term record of service to the TCCB on this and other matters deserves fuller recognition. Instead, what happened in Pakistan would simmer on as some county chairmen began to seek reason to question his right to continue in the chair at TCCB.

Raman now feels that if any good came from the whole sorry saga it is that the concept of independent umpires came a step closer. Resistance to the idea seemed to have been the prevailing attitude at the TCCB. Perhaps the in-built prejudices of imperialism informed attitudes: 'our umpires are the best' had long been one of the unchallenged mantras of English cricket. There was also sympathy for those officiating on the county circuit the peak of whose ambition, to stand in a Lord's Test, might be thwarted. Paradoxically, pressure to introduce neutral officials had first come from Pakistan with Imran Khan his country's most prominent spokesman. With cost an important consideration, independent arbiters for all matches were still some years away, but the first match referees would be appointed within four years, with Raman involved once again. Two further years would pass before the appointment of just one neutral on-field official became ICC policy in Test matches. Gradually steps were being taken to dampen down some of the problems that were afflicting cricket worldwide. On the whole issue Raman, who had experienced his own troubles in India at the start of the decade, had once again long been in the vanguard of progressive thinking: neutral officials were the norm in other major sports, so why not cricket? 'It was something that in the end had to happen,' he now says with some passion, citing the difficulties that arise as soon as any controversy arises. 'With officials from the country involved taking part in it, if there's a problem, then they get locked into the problem of what to do about it. If you have neutral people, then it's up to them to get on and take a neutral decision. My view was that it was something that was absolutely bound to happen in the end, so why don't you get on with it and do it?'

21

'Decisive and visionary or autocratic and misguided'

Difficult times at TCCB

The Pakistan tour over, England were in Australia after Christmas for a single Test at Sydney to mark the bicentenary of white settlement. Forcing Australia to follow on was a high point of the winter, but thereafter only two wickets were captured while 328 runs were piled up. The team then enjoyed a largely incident-free tour of New Zealand. A Broad century and Dilley's best return in Tests put England in the driving seat in the first Test before the home team opted to play out the last day for a draw, after which there were two more drawn games, the second with two days lost to rain after New Zealand had amassed 512 for six. It had been a winter with little to look back on with much pleasure or pride.

Nor did things improve in the summer. Against a West Indies side with Malcolm Marshall in his pomp, there was a false dawn with a 3-0 victory in the ODI series followed by a rare draw in the first Test at Trent Bridge before the next four matches were all comprehensively lost. For Raman, presiding over English cricket, it was not a happy time. Off the field the season got away to a wretched start when Mike Gatting, still England captain, fell into a well-laid gutter press trap after allowing a barmaid to join birthday celebrations in his hotel room. There was no sexual impropriety, but coming so soon after what had happened over the winter, Gatting's ill judgement could not go unpunished. Chairman of selectors Peter May, one of his strongest supporters, felt he had to be suspended from the captaincy. Thoughts that it might be for only one Test did not come to fruition when Gatting defied TCCB wishes and a book was published in his name in which his ghost, Angela Patmore, covered the troubled tour of Pakistan.

So began the summer of four captains as John Emburey took over for two matches before Chris Cowdrey was appointed for the next two. Cowdrey had been leading Kent successfully, but his technical limitations as a batsman were of less interest to the tabloids than the fact that he was the godson of Peter May. In the event injury cut his tenure to a single match, in which he failed miserably as a player and his team lost by ten wickets, before the selectors turned to Graham Gooch. Gooch's involvement with South Africa had earlier counted against him, as had past reluctance to tour, and he had chosen to withdraw from the captaincy of Essex claiming himself to have been a failure with his form as a batsman also impaired. For all his subsequent achievements, Gooch was hardly the obvious answer to the selectors' prayers. Moreover, he had already been saying that he would probably not be available to tour India in the winter. Notwithstanding these reservations, and with his team having squeezed out a first innings lead against West Indies at the Oval, Gooch was retained in preference to Cowdrey for the single Test played against Sri Lanka, which brought a welcome win against less daunting opponents in a match which saw England award four new caps, bringing to 28 the number of players chosen over the course of the summer. Gooch alone had played in all six matches.

As chairman of TCCB Raman was little more than a spectator once the summer was under way, and he was still powerless to influence events directly when the selectors met to choose their captain for the winter's tour to India. As the man in charge, Gooch, having now indicated his willingness to tour, was the obvious, if not ideal, choice. Ossie Wheatley, as chairman of the cricket committee, sat in on the meeting but had no vote or power of veto, though he had the wisdom to suspect that a foolish choice had been made if the first priority was to ensure that the tour took place. Whatever the cricketing merits of the appointment, Gooch had a history of involvement with South Africa, having played for Western Province and led a rebel team back in 1982. To sneak such a player into India, as had happened for the World Cup, was one thing, to have him as captain was another. It was a different situation from the one in which MCC had been able to overrule the selectors' preferred choice of Brian Close to lead the party to tour the West Indies in 1967. Wheatley could only sit by as others made their decision.

There were immediate rumblings from India, just as there had been in 1981 with Cook and Boycott, and there was no certainty that a tour would take place when the selectors sat down on Wednesday 7 September to pick a party of 16. This time Raman was in attendance, as were Ossie Wheatley and Alan Smith, but again they had no vote or right of veto. If Chris Cowdrey had ever been an option as captain – and he had been the logical choice barely a month earlier, even assured by May that captaincy for the tour was the firm plan – he had by now ruled himself out as a possible player with a public attack on Micky Stewart and his own godfather for jettisoning him without a word of explanation. Somehow it typified a period when few players held a regular place in the side and the atmosphere had become one of self-preservation rather than playing for a team. As the deliberations got under way Raman was soon in despair. The selectors' choice of vice-captain was Gooch's bosom pal John Emburey, a fair choice on seniority but hardly forward-looking and a man with a suspect CV on the South Africa front, having served as vice-captain to Gooch on the rebel venture in 1982, which had brought them both a three-year ban from international cricket. 'You must be mad,' Raman remembers himself thinking. His good friend Peter May was following his brief as he understood it: 'to pick the best possible team from a cricketing viewpoint.' Similar words had been flying around at the time of d'Oliveira. What were the selectors up to? 'I very nearly called a special meeting of the TCCB to sack them,' Raman admits.

The party of 16 included eight who had had some involvement with South Africa as player or coach that could be construed as offending the Gleneagles Agreement, but to have both captain and vice-captain as the most prominent was to provoke Indian sentiment too far. Raman had been warned of the dangers that summer by N.K.P. Salve, an immediate past president of the Indian Board of Control and a serving minister in Rajiv Gandhi's cabinet. With Gooch having spoken openly about a contract he had signed to play for Western Province before the possibility of captaining England arose, the portents were not good. Within 48 hours of the selection meeting came official word from India that the tour was off. The selected players were paid their tour fee to sit at home.

In November Peter May resigned. At a time when other international teams were getting stronger, England were low in players of proven class, and he had had a torrid time striving to find eleven good enough to win. For Alan Lee in *The Times*, writing some weeks before his resignation, May was thrice culpable of disposing of captains without once sitting down and explaining why. It was an unforgiveable catalogue of failure, and he hoped it would 'hasten the departure of May from a job for which he was never well suited and in which he has now, by common consent, outstayed his welcome.'

If there was one positive outcome to the saga it was in bringing closer to resolution the problems of players exercising their rights to play in South Africa. That winter Raman was making good use of his influence as TCCB representative at the ICC meeting. It led to what Bill Frindall, in his *Playfair* editorial, described as 'the most vital legislation in the history of the International Cricket Conference.' He went on to write: 'No praise can be too high for the tireless efforts and determination of the TCCB's chairman, Raman Subba Row, to negotiate a set of ground rules to cover players' contact with South Africa which were acceptable to all ICC members.' Frindall hoped that Raman's efforts would help to 'save Test cricket from further expedient meddling from politicians.'

With those running cricket in Pakistan and India invariably closely tied to the governments of their countries, it meant that acceptable ground rules inevitably hit hard at the many English county professionals who regularly looked for a winter's coaching in South Africa – if they had any aspirations to play for England, it meant waving goodbye to them. In the words of Mike Procter, 'The interests of English players were sacrificed to keep international cricket alive.' It was disheartening for those who had sought to take cricket into the townships of Soweto at a time when many white cricketers were doing what they could to demonstrate a will to bring multi-racial cricket to their country in their bid to regain membership of the ICC.

On the domestic front Raman had taken the chance to review the management structure under which England teams operated. Together with Wheatley and Alan Smith, he proposed a more professional set up with a full-time paid chairman of the England committee, to whom Micky Stewart would report and who would chair selection meetings. He found in Ted Dexter a man with similar ideas to his own and a willingness to take the job on. He had expected to share his thinking with county chairmen before any formal announcement. The concept had been exposed at their December meeting, and Derbyshire chairman Chris Middleton has gone on record that he was told in strict confidence at a subsequent meeting at the Oval to discuss the South Africa question that the man Raman had found was Dexter. Any chance for the chairmen to endorse the choice at their next meeting was scuppered by a leak that led the press to Dexter's doorstep. County chairmen were not best pleased to hear for the first time of another important TCCB decision when they saw Dexter being interviewed on television. Ammunition was being stored up by those who felt that Raman was too independent in the way he conducted himself.

There was one important change in the way Dexter's new regime would work: in the future the chairman of the cricket committee would have the right of veto over the choice of captain. The summer's visitors were the Australians, determined as ever to regain the Ashes and led by a captain, Alan Border, who had developed a new toughness after the traumas his men had suffered in 1985. Who might best lead England if Border's men were to be thwarted? Micky Stewart had no doubts. For him Mike Gatting remained by far the best option. He found Dexter prepared to support his preference. This came as an undoubted disappointment to others at TCCB, where there had been a presumption that Dexter might opt for a man more in his own image. Ossie Wheatley then chose to exercise his right of veto. In this he was supported by Raman. For Wheatley it was a simple matter. The put-up incident with the barmaid was of no consequence, but what had happened in Pakistan was unacceptable. 'It's a simple principle,' he says. 'An England captain should never be seen arguing with an umpire, not in any circumstances.' Going on to stress that there are other avenues to pursue when disenchanted with an umpire's performance, he is keenly aware of the importance of the example top players set in all sport. 'Children imitate what they see done on television.'

The veto was a big blow to Stewart, as was the subsequent rejection of Gooch in favour of David Gower, who had not played in South Africa and who had avoided any revelations about his private life. There was just one problem with the squeaky clean man foisted on the England team manager: Stewart and Gower could never forge a successful partnership. The laid back Gower represented all that Stewart had striven to overcome. He was going back beyond square one. Yet the pretence that Gower was their first choice was maintained, the restored captain not learning of Dexter and Stewart's preference for Gatting until the series was over.

Of that summer's six Tests four were lost and two drawn, both of them after the loss of playing time with Australia well on top. Twenty-nine players were used, five of them new caps, four old lags recalled including a now fading Botham, and 20 who had also been in and out of the side the previous summer. Only the captain and new wicket-keeper, Jack Russell, played in all six Tests. To cap it all, mid-way through the summer Mike Gatting and 15 other England qualified cricketers decided that the lure of the South African rand was a more attractive proposition than the prospect of playing for their country. The newly agreed ICC protocol meant that, by 'pursuing their trade', as they liked to describe it, they were turning their backs on any chance of playing for England for five years. Half of the party had taken part in the Ashes series including several with whom it was hoped that England's future lay such as Kim Barnett, Matthew Maynard and Paul Jarvis. For Raman it was another season where everything seemed to have gone wrong with English cricket.

What was he, as the supremo, to do about it? His own initiative on the international front had rebounded on him with the rebel tour, while on the domestic front, as a man who likes to see his ideas translated into action, he was battling with a structure that has continued to bedevil the game. Put at its simplest, the interests of the England team and those of the first-class counties do not always align. Raman was concerned that three-day cricket had led to a formula that he summed up as 'You have one day, I'll have the second, then we'll carve up the third.' He felt this was no way to produce Test cricketers. He had therefore welcomed the report from a recently conducted enquiry by Charles Palmer, in which some four-day matches had been proposed. Only with four-day cricket, he felt, would batsmen have the chance to build innings in the manner required in Test matches, while bowlers would likewise have to become more resourceful to earn their wickets. Palmer also recommended returning to uncovered pitches, for the three-day games at least, once play had been called off for the day. This latter initiative lasted just one season, 1987, and was a somewhat half-hearted trial with the creases left covered, thereby allowing pace bowlers to maintain a sure foothold and take advantage of conditions that had at one time been what spinners were waiting for.

Four-day matches were a more serious proposition. Palmer had recommended eight in a total match programme of 24. In true style this had to be watered down: 1988 saw a championship of 22 matches with just six played over four days, three at each end of the season. It was at least a start, but Raman wanted more and he was soon battling with the counties, hearing arguments that Hobbs and Hutton had adapted well enough from three-day to five-day cricket, while the counties' main complaint was that the week divided up unsatisfactorily for the selling of corporate packages, and it became harder to give members a weekend with two days' cricket. Moreover, a championship programme trimmed to 16 matches would make it more difficult to take cricket round the county, as Yorkshire and a few others had always liked to do.

Raman's other concern was the quality of pitches. In his brief time as a Surrey player he had seen them doctored to suit Laker and Lock, and there had been other instances in more recent times. There seemed to be wide agreement that pitches were getting steadily worse. Graham Gooch was one who was emphatic about this: 'The pitches this year are very much worse than at any stage in my career. You go round the country and you expect to be batting on a minefield. It does absolutely nothing for your form and confidence when you have to play a Test match after that.' The climate was right for the imposition of the strong penalties Raman had always favoured. For the 1989 season TCCB approved a scheme whereby a county risked a 25-point penalty for the production of a sub-standard pitch. A small cadre of inspectors were recruited to make visits where the umpires reported dissatisfaction. In the first season a poor pitch cost Essex the Championship, perhaps harshly as the offending strip had been prepared not by the county's ground staff but by the local council at Southend. It was a potential nail in the coffin for outgrounds.

By the autumn of 1989 Raman had known he was on borrowed time as chairman of TCCB. The scars of his experience in Pakistan – 'rewarding total anarchy' – were never allowed to heal, and the decision to appoint Ted Dexter to his England role had also led to complaints that there had been no semblance of consultation before the name was in the papers. With many county chairmen at odds with the causes Raman was espousing, their concerns were made clear to Alan Smith. He consulted Doug Insole, a former chairman, who recalls that it was 'not one of my happier days' when he and Smith visited the Oval to address the matter with Raman. They had given no warning that their visit was to convey the county chairmen's message that it was time for him to go. Only by agreeing not to have his name go forward again was Raman enabled to retain office into the 1990 season. That he had become a divisive figure was fully appreciated by Alan Lee. Neatly capturing the two sides to a coin that has always characterised Raman in his mission to serve English cricket, the cricket correspondent of *The Times* wrote: 'Some regard him as decisive and visionary; others as autocratic and misguided'

Raman's successor had been known since the December meeting in 1989, when Northamptonshire chairman Frank Chamberlain was the counties' choice to take over for 1991. A businessman with a family firm in the shoe trade, Chamberlain was High Sherriff for his county at the time he took office, soon to become Deputy Lieutenant. A freeman of the City of London and a regional director of the National Westminster Bank, his love of country pursuits completed the list of appropriate establishment credentials. As with most of his fellow chairmen, Chamberlain's playing credentials were modest though he could claim some first-class experience: six championship matches as a batsman for Northants in 1946 had brought him 67 runs with a top score of 13. Chamberlain was the kind of English gentleman with whom most of the chairmen will have felt instinctively comfortable, and he had no axes to grind. 'He was a neutral figure, which is what people wanted,' says Doug Insole, 'someone with no strong views.' They could all breathe more easily. 'The pace wouldn't have been so intense,' says a county chairman, 'and it would certainly have been a quieter life for the chief executive!' For the editor of *Wisden*, it was 'a clear decision not to have an activist in charge.'

His last year gave Raman one final chance to win his battle for a championship of 16 four-day matches. Despite Dexter, Wheatley and Stewart all being strongly in favour, as Peter May had been before them, and with known support from the county captains, it was still a forlorn cause. The county chairmen knew that their members would not be happy to lose so many days of cricket, and their treasurers would be fearing for the viability of the fourth day. At the March meeting the motion was lost by 14 votes to four. A later bid at a special meeting to increase the number of four-day games to eight saw the counties and MCC split evenly at nine each. Raman as chairman with a casting vote could have had his way, but he observed the convention that the status quo should prevail: for 1991 the format would not change. He still remained confident that four-day cricket would come. Two years later the motion was carried. In 1992 the Championship saw its last three-day match and from 1993 the fixture programme comprised 16 four-day matches.

The subjective nature of pitch assessment would continue to make this a festering issue for years to come, though the summer of 1990 was marked instead by warm weather, an experimental ball with minimal seam and batsmen gorging themselves to set a championship record of 38.72 runs per wicket, more than eight higher than the average over the previous decade. And those runs came at a good pace: never in the history of the Championship had the rate of scoring been faster. At both Lord's and the Oval new records were set for the highest individual score on the ground, by Graham Gooch and Neil Fairbrother. The run feast also allayed some of the fears of blank fourth days: despite the sunshine, half of the championship matches still ended in draws. The summer had left Raman's successors with many problems still to address, but with pitches starting to improve and the prospect of universal four-day cricket edging closer, he could feel he was leaving the chair at TCCB with English cricket in a better state than he had found it, albeit it would not be long before he was publishing his views that cricket's new found money was not well directed to restoring the fortunes of the England team.

Raman had waited until his successor had retired before taking up the cudgels. In January 1995, as England reeled to defeat in Australia, he was bemoaning the fact that cricket as structured in England so ill prepared those aspiring to play for their country. Writing to *The Times*, he maintained that 'vested interests had blocked progressive thinking.' His letter continued: 'Ailing organisations don't mend themselves; normally a financial yardstick comes into play. Regrettably, in this case expanding revenue from commercial sources is only exacerbating the problem. More and more cash is being distributed to fund more and more mediocrity as well as expensive overseas players. Someone must break this vicious circle of mismanagement and create a new accountable structure. The need is all the greater when time has already run out.'

A year later he was writing on the same theme, acknowledging his overuse of the 'turkeys not voting for Christmas' analogy. He hoped for a new structure for domestic cricket, but still feared that 'even the long-awaited England Cricket Board will never vote to reduce their own status for our international benefit.' Eventually Raman would see Lord MacLaurin, as chairman of the new ECB, battle to implement some of the changes Raman might have wished to see imposed, a two division championship and central contracts among them. Yet MacLaurin, like Raman, would leave office frustrated by the intransigence of the counties and admitting defeat that his attempts to put England cricket's house in order had only partially succeeded.

22

'I need men I can trust'

International match referee

Whatever may have been the rights and wrongs of those who sought to see him relinquish the chair at TCCB, Raman had remained true to his ideals and, as ever, looking to move the game forward and put it on a more professional footing. The award of a CBE was richly deserved when it came in the New Year's honours list for 1991 alongside one for Test Match Special's Brian Johnston. In the same year Raman was made an honorary member of MCC.

At Buckingham Palace
Alistair, Anne, Raman, Christopher

Responsibility for the management of national cricket behind him, Raman was still pumping out papers for the consideration of those running affairs at the Oval, but it was on the international scene that he was next to become most heavily involved. Prior to 1989 the International Cricket Conference had always been run from Lord's with the incumbent president of MCC as chairman. It was a relic of colonial times, and a practice that gave the office-holder little time to find his feet before his term was up. From 1989, when the Conference became the International Cricket Council, a chairman was installed whose term could run for four years, soon to become three. The new arrangement was one of the recommendations stemming from the deliberations of a working party engaged on the project for over three years – under the chairmanship of Raman. Among their other recommendations was that the historic power of the founder nations, England and Australia, should be diluted. The veto either country had been able to exercise was now available only if they acted in unison.

England were not immediately to surrender chairmanship of the new ICC. With the power of appointment still lying in the gift of MCC's president, Field Marshal Lord Bramall's nomination of Colin Cowdrey meant that it was still in establishment hands. But Cowdrey was a man who shared Raman's passionate belief that there was much needing to be put right with the international game. The list of concerns that dominated ICC meetings included slow over rates, endless short-pitched fast bowling and, above all, a decline in player behaviour. Also about to come fully to the boil was ball tampering. Having neutral umpires for international matches had long been a cause Raman had championed as part of the answer to just these issues, and it had been debated by the ICC as far back as 1982. Plans were now more firmly afoot to introduce independent officials, though it would be 1993 before the first ICC appointed neutral umpire took the field, initially standing alongside a locally appointed colleague. However, a forerunner to this would be match referees.

A naturally cautious man, Cowdrey knew the introduction of referees would not be plain sailing. Umpires might think their authority was being usurped; he needed to show it was being strengthened because they would be backed up in a way that might not always happen with partisan controlling bodies. Those bodies, too, might feel their rights were being infringed, when an outsider disciplined one of their players. Whatever the reservations, Cowdrey knew he had strong support from most of the major cricketing nations, who had grown tired of seeing the game's values and traditions abused by petulant players – and there was no shortage of incidents to which they could point from recent international matches.

The next question for Cowdrey was deciding who should be appointed. Here he got his head together with MCC secretary John Stephenson, who still served in the same capacity with ICC. They concluded that they needed men who had played the game at an appropriate level – all should be former Test players. There were also social implications – the referees would be expected to mix easily with the host nation's administrators. Cowdrey wanted to start with men he knew he could trust to bring these qualities to the task. And he needed people with the time to do the job. Those chosen had in common that they were Oxbridge men of his immediate generation and all had gone on to a substantial career in county cricket: Peter May, Mike Smith, Donald Carr and Raman. All except Raman had captained England. It was easily portrayed as an extension of the English establishment controlling cricket, but there was sound sense in Cowdrey going for men he knew well. And for Raman it came at the right moment in life when, approaching 60, he had decided to retire from Management Public Relations.

The first Test to have an international referee was at Brisbane on 29 November 1991, when Australia and India began a five-Test series. Mike Smith took the first two matches with Peter May presiding over the next three. Meanwhile Donald Carr had been to Pakistan to oversee three matches against Sri Lanka, in the last of which Shakoor Rana returned to the Test arena for the first time since his spat with Mike Gatting. He and his partner, Khalid Aziz, managed to uphold what was then the world record of 14 lbw decisions, with six going against Pakistan batsmen in their first innings. With a non-English referee required when Graham Gooch's team toured New Zealand, Cowdrey turned to Peter Burge of Australia.

Raman's first appointments came in the West Indies in April 1992, when he officiated for three ODIs followed by the match that marked South Africa's historic return to Test cricket after 22 years in exile. If there was one man for whom this match had special significance it was Raman. To see South Africa back in the international fold, a South Africa in which a man of Indian parentage could move without barriers, was the consummation of his dreams. Years of forlorn pleading had passed with the South African Cricket Board doing all they could to implement multi-racial cricket in a country where the law was against them. Sometimes defying their own government in taking coaching into the townships, the board felt they had done all that was asked of them only to be rebuffed by the international community. Then the barriers came down with dramatic suddenness. In January 1991, at its first ever meeting away from Lord's, the ICC had 'noted' that there was a single ruling body for the country's cricket. The newly formed United Cricket Board of South Africa was to assume control of all cricket played in South Africa without regard to the traditional segregation by colour. On 11 February, even as Mike Gatting's rebel team was touring the country, Nelson Mandela ended 27 years in prison. By this time the ANC had been legitimised, and at the ICC's annual meeting at Lord's on 10 July India proposed and Australia seconded the return to international cricket of one of the ICC's founder members.

For Raman there was reward at last for all those hopeful telephone calls from Ali Bacher and he could also reflect on the meetings he had had with his long-standing friend Alan Rae, who been dealt the hardest political hand of all. With the iniquities of the slave trade as a backdrop to West Indian thinking, Alan Rae represented not one country but five that contributed players to a 'federation' that came together for no purpose other than playing cricket – and there was a total of 14 governments entitled to a say in what official policy should be. Rae, a successful opening batsman in the West Indies team that toured England in 1950, was a barrister, of whom it was said that he ignored his practice in the cause of cricket. After serving his native Jamaica, he was president of the West Indies Cricket Board of Control in the years leading into the return of South Africa to international cricket, and his task was always the harder for heading an impecunious board whose ability to reward its cricketers fell far short of other countries, let alone the riches offered to those prepared to be paid in rands. For those West Indians who chose to ignore the ban on playing in South Africa, the ultimate penalties went far beyond being banished from the international cricket field. Ostracised by their own communities, several soon fell on hard times, while others were obliged to make new lives for themselves away from the Caribbean. Small wonder, therefore, that West Indies should have been the hardest nut to crack when the motion to re-admit South Africa to the ICC was on the table.

Just what the long years of isolation had meant came home to Raman when he attended a ceremony before the Test match. 'I had Jackie McGlew on one side and Everton Weekes on the other and it took me a while before I realised that they had never met. Rather sheepishly I introduced them to each other.'

The three ODIs had all been won comfortably by the home side, but the single Test, played at Bridgetown, Barbados, proved to be a splendid contest that ended with South Africa, eight wickets in hand, needing only 79 to win on the final day. Swept aside by the fine pace bowling of Curtly Ambrose and Courtney Walsh, they fell 53 short. The match drew a disappointingly sparse crowd, as the locals sought to register their indignation at the omission of local fast bowler Anderson Cummins. Raman had had no need to exercise his disciplinary role, but the match was not without controversy. In West Indies' second innings, Brian Lara, in completing a leg glance, had dislodged a bail, but neither umpire saw it happen. The incident caused a prolonged on-field discussion before the batsman was given not out. Though it was clear from television to Raman and the stand-by umpire that Lara was out, there was nothing they could do to intervene. 'The umpires were perfectly correct to give the ruling they did if they were unsighted,' Raman said at close of play. 'There is no doubt, though, that this incident will bring further discussions about the possibility of a third, outside official having the power to intervene if needed.' Ironically, Lara was out shortly afterwards, caught by the wicket-keeper when it appeared from television that the ball had brushed only his pad.

Initially all referees were picked by Cowdrey, but very soon countries were invited to put forward their own nominees. Over the first two years many distinguished former Test cricketers were called with captains well represented. West Indies led the way with Everton Weekes, Clyde Walcott, Conrad Hunte, Clive Lloyd, Cammie Smith, Jackie Hendriks and Deryck Murray; from Australia Burge was joined by Bob Cowper; from New Zealand came John Reid and Frank Cameron; from India Sunil Gavaskar, the Nawab of Pataudi and former Test umpire Srinivas Venkataraghavan; from Pakistan Javed Burki, Asif Iqbal and Zaheer Abbas. South Africa's former captains Jackie McGlew and Peter van der Merwe joined the list, while Sri Lanka's sole representative was a man who would outstay them all, Ranjan Madugalle, now comfortably the most experienced of all match referees. A young man when he started, by early 2017 he had covered 175 Test matches, more than twice as many as his nearest rival, and he comfortably tops the ODI list as well.

Cowdrey had always expected that the number of referees would quickly thin down, and even with a vastly increased programme of international matches, the panel in 2017 consists of just seven men. There were inevitable teething problems as referees felt their way on such issues as the extent to which they should step in or only act on an umpire's report and in the severity of punishments handed out. It was not until the fifteenth match under the new system that the first disciplinary action was recorded, Conrad Hunte fining Pakistan bowler Aqib Javed 50% of his match fee for an unholy spat with umpire Roy Palmer at Old Trafford. This was accompanied by a reprimand for his captain, Javed Miandad, and another slap on the wrist for manager Intikhab Alam for speaking to the press. Yet the action taken by Hunte was not free from criticism, the wrath of England captain Graham Gooch being incurred when the referee saw it as his duty to speak to *both* teams.

Raman was to follow Hunte's lead the ensuing winter, when he flew to Australia for a trip spanning Christmas that would take in the first two Tests of what was always expected to be an aggressively fought series with West Indies. Sandwiched between the Tests were eight ODIs in a triangular tournament also involving Pakistan, all of which Raman was to cover. He encountered trouble in the first Test, in which he fined Allan Border, the Australian captain, 50% of his match fee for unacceptable language to umpire Steve Randell, language that Border sought to pass off as 'a cheeky remark'. Raman had considered suspension, but was advised against this course of action by Cowdrey. In the same match Raman fined Merv Hughes 10% of his match fee for dissent and abusive language to an umpire.

As Border had initially chosen not to turn up for his hearing, Raman may be considered to have acted leniently. Certainly this was how Donald Carr's actions appeared when he merely reprimanded the same pair of offenders in the fifth Test at Perth. The early days of match refereeing drew criticism from some quarters for reluctance to take strong action in stamping out boorish behaviour, with some of the English choices seeming to favour a softer touch. Donald Carr lasted three Test series, Mike Smith only two, while Peter May's first three Test were his last. So, as the thinning out process took place, only Raman remained of Cowdrey's original nominations.

Over the next nine years he would enjoy undertaking a job that took him around the world, with Anne sometimes able to accompany him. From 1993 Raman's Test match schedule, with starting dates, was:

> April 1993: West Indies v Pakistan
> February 1994: New Zealand v Pakistan
> March 1994: New Zealand v India
> November 1995: India v West Indies
> January 1997: Australia v West Indies
> February 1997: South Africa v Australia
> November 1997: Pakistan v West Indies
> January 1998: Sri Lanka v Zimbabwe
> March 1999: West Indies v Australia
> December 1999: New Zealand v West Indies
> February 2000: India v South Africa
> November 2000: Bangladesh v India
> December 2000: South Africa v Sri Lanca
> November 2001: Sri Lanca v West Indies

On most assignments Raman would be engaged with a series of ODIs or a triangular tournament running alongside the Tests, but there were other separate ODI assignments. In the autumns of 1994 and 1995 it was triangular series, first in India then Sharjah. In February 1996 the World Cup took Raman to Pakistan and India, where he was chosen to referee the final in Calcutta. In October 1998 it was a tournament in Bangladesh, then the World Cup in England the following summer. In March 2000 he was back in Sharjah; later that year he was off to Kenya for the ICC Knock out

Cup. Then his last Test match assignment, in Sri Lanka, brought Raman his final ODI matches in the LG Abans Trophy.

Though refereeing gave Raman the chance to catch up with his many cricketing friends across the world, his visit to New Zealand in 1994 was punctuated by the sad news from England that his brother Stanley was unlikely to live for many more days. The two brothers, who remained close throughout life, were able to enjoy a final telephone conversation before Stanley died on 28 February, the final day of New Zealand's third Test against Pakistan at Christchurch. With a series of ODIs to follow, then hot on its heels a Test and five ODIs against India, Raman was expecting to be kept occupied in New Zealand until early April. It was thanks to the kindness of his good friend Peter Burge, who flew in from Australia, that Raman was able to be back in England for 48 hours to attend Stanley's funeral on 9 March.

By 2017 only one English nominee, Chris Broad, second to Madugalle with 82 in the overall list, had refereed more Tests than Raman's 41, which place him in eleventh position overall. His 119 ODIs take Raman to ninth spot. These 160 international matches brought Raman eleven recorded instances where he was obliged to deal with unacceptable behaviour, a strike rate lower than most colleagues standing in a comparable number of matches. He certainly didn't shirk from his duty in the face of big names. Brian Lara was fined 50% of his match fee with a one-match suspension for dissent over a stumping decision, only the second time a player had been debarred in this way from playing in a future match. A spit in the direction of an opposing player by Glenn McGrath activated a suspended 30% match fee fine. Pakistan's Aamir Sohail was suspended for one ODI after twice telling an umpire to look at the replay screen. For Ian Healy it was two matches for more serious dissent. David Houghton, as coach of Zimbabwe, was banned from a similar number for public criticisms of the umpires.

To Raman, more important than handing out punishments was conveying to a player the seriousness of his misdeed, ensuring that there would be no repeat. He even recalls one instance of receiving a letter of thanks for his strictures and advice. Over the decade in which he was involved Raman saw player behaviour begin to improve, though he came to wonder at the value of financial penalties, increasingly irrelevant to the game's big earners. Though not in favour of a penalty that would adjust the score of a match, he saw suspension as the threat that was most likely to ensure players respected the spirit of the game.

Raman's refereeing days preceded the right of players to challenge on-field decisions. Player reviews were still some years away, perhaps further than they might have been had the ever forward-looking Raman been driving the decision-making within the ICC. 'I think we should be making use of television,' he said shortly after retiring. 'If the umpire is not sure about anything, he should not be afraid to ask for its help. There are times when the whole world knows ten seconds later that the umpire has made a big mistake. That can be avoided.'

There was an occasion in Guyana when Raman decided to take the law into his own hands to ensure that equity prevailed. With West Indies requiring two runs to win an ODI off the final ball, Pakistan's fielders were distracted by celebrating local supporters storming onto the outfield as the runs were being completed. Raman stepped in to declare the second run invalid, thereby decreeing that the match and, as it happened, the series ended tied.

During Raman's time as a referee the first rumblings of match-fixing were starting to come to light. He was on duty in India for what were to be the last Test matches played by Hansie Cronje and the ODIs that followed them. 'There were strange things that I couldn't understand,' he said shortly afterwards. 'It was the start of match-fixing, which actually went back to 1993/4 during a tournament involving India, West Indies and New Zealand. There was evidence of it then. I spoke to the captains. The ICC should have tackled things more professionally, but they didn't.'

By 1993 the chairmanship of Colin Cowdrey had run its course. His successor, now elected by the other ICC members, was Clyde Walcott. Sir Clyde, as he would become in 1994, was the first non-English man to hold international cricket's highest office, later to be styled president. The members had had one alternative candidate to consider – Raman. But the time was ripe for an end to England's monopoly of running the game across the world and he was unsurprisingly defeated. Sir Clyde Walcott was to prove an able leader of the international game, but had the members' choice been Raman who knows what his visionary qualities might have brought.

Raman's days on the international scene were over once he had passed his seventieth birthday, but he had one final contribution to make to the game as he concerned himself with one of the ongoing problems of English cricket – the quality of pitches. For a few years, initially working closely with Harry Brind, Raman was one of ECB's pitch inspectors, called out to assess strips where umpires expressed dissatisfaction or wickets appeared to be falling too quickly. Reports of his incursions suggest that he was not too easily persuaded that there was much amiss with a pitch that could not be accounted for by poor batting. As his son Alistair sagely points out, there was something symbolically appropriate that his father's final contributions to cricket should have been close to the game's grass roots.

23

'Not just a great opponent but one of my dearest friends'

The final analysis

On 29 January 2017 Raman's family gathered at his South Croydon home to celebrate the 85th birthday of a much loved husband, father and grandfather. Round the table that day with Raman and Anne were their younger son Alistair and his wife Laura with their four children, Emily, Thomas, Max and Jake. Alistair is senior partner in Farebrother, real estate advisers and chartered surveyors. He is a freeman of the City of London, a member of the Court of The Worshipful Company of Chartered Surveyors and a trustee of The Garden Bridge Trust. His children are now mostly launched into adult life. Emily works as a merchandiser for Andrew Winch Design, internationally renowned yacht designers. Thomas is a property investment surveyor with

Raman at 85

Savills. Max is spending a gap year teaching in Australia prior to going to Bournemouth University to study sports business management, while Jake is preparing for A levels at Cranleigh School.

Unable to join the party was Alistair's elder brother Christopher, who lives with his wife Karen in the Middle East. They have three sons: Alex works for a firm in the City selling computer software to banks; Nick is a captain in the British Army; and Rory is reading Estate Management at Nottingham Trent University. Raman and Anne's daughter Michelle keeps herself busy living in Suffolk. She has one son, Harry, who works in asset management with Goldman Sachs.

The man whose life was being celebrated retains little of the agility of his youth, seldom venturing far from his home, but the writing of this book has provided ample evidence of the hospitality for which Anne and Raman are renowned. As we have reminisced, Raman's over-generous hand with the wine bottle has perfectly complemented the platefuls of sandwiches and pies Anne can be trusted to bring us.

The hesitant undergraduate and the once shy young amateur who first joined the boisterous Northants dressing room soon matured to earn a reputation as a gregarious mixer, recalled with respect and affection by those with whom he has enjoyed the post-match bonhomie that characterised club cricket of his generation. He has been one who cherishes reunions. His returns to Northampton, no longer practical, were always awaited with pleasure by those he once led on the field. So, too, the annual get togethers of college friends from his time at Cambridge, and those close by at Whitgift, where to speak with Dr Christopher Barnett is to understand what Raman has given to his old school.

Though it may no longer be easy for Raman to get out and about, he is seldom short of friends paying a visit to revive memories of earlier years. It might have been John Barrett – 'I used to play against him in my schooldays,' Raman says, not clarifying whether they had met on the cricket field or across the net at tennis. I am told that he has just called round accompanied by his charming wife Angela, Wimbledon champion in 1961. Anne's principal game has also been tennis. Her days on the court are over, but the cards are always out awaiting the next four of bridge, the game Raman taught her years ago and the one she fears must once have put his degree in jeopardy. Now the Barretts can provide competition at the card table with a few reminiscences of trips together to the tennis championships. Who had called round the time before? It might have been Robin Marlar. Or was it Sidath Wettimuny?

Anne's involvement with charitable and other work ensures a busy diary. She is a trustee of Queen Elizabeth's Foundation for Disabled People. She was also a committee member of the Women's National Cancer Control Campaign, of which Judith Chalmers was chairman. The arts play a big part in Anne's life. She is a keen member of NADFAS (the National Association of Decorative & Fine Arts Societies), having helped to start a society in Croydon many years ago. She is also involved with her local Probus ladies' club, and then there are her flowers – you won't keep her away from Chelsea each year!

Nearly thirty years ago Anne was a leading figure in a small group who started the Lady Taverners, a charity that came into being when Margaret Thatcher became prime minister. A woman in high office caused a headache for the all-male Lord's Taverners, whose practice had always been to install the prime minister of the day as a member. Confronted by a female, the hierarchy rose to the challenge, ingeniously inviting Mrs Thatcher to become Lady Taverner Number One, a position she happily accepted. In April 2017, as this book was about to go to the printers, to delight of the Subba Row family, came news that their connection with the Taverners was to be reinforced with the election of Alistair as a trustee.

With Lady Taverners prominent in the parties, Anne has arranged many overseas trips over the past twenty-five years, particularly recalling one in which some thirty-six women went on safari accompanied by just one man, David Shepherd. Not the differently spelled bishop, not the umpire but the wild life artist! His wife Avril is a great friend of Anne.

The telephone – and its easy reach around the world – helps Anne keep in touch with the wide circle of friends she and Raman have built up through his involvement with cricket as player and administrator. 'There are not many baddies in cricket,' Raman has always said, and for him and Anne friends have come from wherever the game is played, son Alistair remembering a childhood with Uncle Jackie (Hendriks) or Uncle Alan (Rae or Davidson) and others from India, Australia and New Zealand as regular guests. These friends in turn speak of Anne's warmth and almost unparalleled hospitality and kindness. 'My daughter wanted to join a finishing school in London,' says Madhav Apte. 'Anne took her to see it and looked after her for a year when she went there.' Alan Davidson is one who spurns hotels to stay with Raman and Anne. Of Raman, whose wicket he captured five times in that far off summer of 1961, he says that he was 'not just a great opponent, but he is one of my dearest friends – nearly a brother.' Alan's recollections include the wider family, and he speaks of Stanley with great affection: 'If you were looking for a brother, you couldn't have had a better.' To Gopi Gopinath

Lady Taverners 21st anniversary lunch, April 2008

Back: Sylvia Tidy, Jean Ratcliff, Colleen Rumsey, Bette Hill, Anita Harris, Maggie Smith
Front: Dame Norma Major, Rosa Tidy, Lady Myra Secombe, Barbara Upsdell, Anne
Subba Row, Betty Surridge, Baroness Thatcher, Jane Sheridan, Norma Pearce, Joan
Morecambe, Denise Horne, Judith Chalmers, Rachael Heyhoe-Flint, Carole Overton

Raman is 'someone who makes friends with anyone, anywhere' and Gopi goes on to say he once went searching for him only to find him locked in conversation with a total stranger he had met in the road.

There is much for them to talk about with a game that has seen so many changes, many for the better, some more questionable. Yet for all that Raman has given to the game, his many friends have expressed their disappointment, even anger, that he has not been more fully honoured at Lord's and the Oval. In 1980 Peter May became the first post-war Cambridge Blue to serve as president of MCC. Since that date a further 16 light blues have held the office, four of them as well as May having played in Cambridge sides alongside Raman. Over this 38-year period just two Oxford Blues have presided over MCC: Colin Cowdrey and Charles Fry. Among conspicuous absentees from those who have graced Fenner's and gone on to devote many years to the service of the game are Raman and Ossie Wheatley, two men who have consistently taken a long-term and constructive view of cricket's needs. In the curious world of the governance of English cricket, they have devoted their time wholeheartedly to the new regime of TCCB/ECB, where others have retained feet in both camps. Hence of those who have headed up the Board, Charles Palmer and Dennis Silk came as recent past presidents of MCC, while George Mann, Doug Insole and David Morgan were all given the honour of presidency after many years of service with the Board.

It fell to Raman and Wheatley to clip the wings of MCC, to recommend and eventually see implemented a reduction in the direct influence of cricket's former rulers, thereby enabling money to flow into the game through initiatives that would have provoked rumblings in the proverbial celestial circles among those whose word was once law. Lord Harris, Pelham Warner, Gubby Allen – what might they have said of logos painted on the outfield and the razzmatazz of Twenty20 cricket? Raman, it must be remembered, was a true visionary paving the way to much that has made cricket prosperous, and visionaries may have to tread on a few corns to achieve their ends. Moreover, where there will always be opposition to change, Raman was dealing not so much with change as upheaval.

Those who have known him well have acknowledged that Raman may have been politically astute but he was always principled. He has fought his corner for what he believed was right, seldom for what might serve his own personal cause. In the process he has taken decisions others might not have and he has acted with an authority some have maintained he did not have. It was his fate to have his hand on the tiller at a time when English cricket was at a low ebb with challenges to be met on and off the field, all with a hostile media hovering in hopeful expectation of a false step. He may not always have been right in how he addressed the challenges, but he was driven by a sense of purpose that some have seen as stubbornness. Friends have noticed that, because he has always cared with passion about the causes he has espoused, he has found it difficult to set differences aside when leaving the committee room. It has been said, by some of his greatest friends, that he bears grudges. Yet the balance sheet is surely strongly in his favour. If one looks at Raman's contribution in his years as an administrator, to the changes that he pioneered to improve the game's structure and finances, it could be argued that he has played as great a part in taking English cricket forward as any man alive.

181

A BRIEF STATISTICAL DIGEST

BATTING AND FIELDING IN FIRST-CLASS CRICKET

HOME

Year	M	I	NO	Runs	HS	Ave	100	50	Ct
1951	12	16	3	294	77*	22.61	-	1	10
1952	14	19	3	661	94	41.31	-	5	10
1953	30	46	10	1823	146*	50.63	4	13	22
1954	28	41	7	982	117*	28.88	1	5	25
1955	27	41	5	1384	260*	38.44	4	5	18
1956	3	4	-	177	108	44.25	1	-	-
1957	6	10	1	224	70	24.88	-	1	6
1958	32	48	9	1810	300	46.41	5	7	18
1959	27	46	5	1917	183*	46.75	6	10	20
1960	18	32	5	1503	147*	55.66	4	6	9
1961	26	50	4	1710	137	37.17	3	8	22
1964	1	2	-	66	61	33.00	-	1	-
Total	**224**	**355**	**52**	**12551**	**300**	**41.42**	**28**	**62**	**160**

OVERSEAS

Year	M	I	NO	Runs	HS	Ave	100	50	Ct
1953/54 *(I)*	14	18	6	512	77*	42.66	-	4	6
1958/59 *(A/NZ)*	10	15	3	414	83	34.50	-	3	2
1959/60 *(WI)*	9	14	3	598	110	54.36	2	3	4
1961/62 *(I/P)*	2	3	1	103	51	51.50	-	1	4
1967/68 *(I)*	1	2	-	4	4	2.00	-	-	-
Total	**36**	**52**	**13**	**1631**	**110**	**41.82**	**2**	**11**	**16**
Total	**260**	**407**	**65**	**14182**	**300**	**41.46**	**30**	**73**	**176**

BATTING AND FIELDING IN TEST CRICKET

Year	M	I	NO	Runs	HS	Ave	100	50	Ct
1958 *(NZ)*	1	1	-	9	9	9.00	-	-	1
1959 *(Ind)*	1	1	-	94	94	94.00	-	1	-
1959/60 *(WI)*	2	4	-	162	100	40.50	1	-	-
1960 *(SA)*	4	6	1	251	90	50.20	-	2	2
1961 *(Aus)*	5	10	-	468	137	46.80	2	1	2
Total	**13**	**22**	**1**	**984**	**137**	**46.85**	**3**	**4**	**5**

BOWLING IN FIRST-CLASS CRICKET

HOME

Year	Overs	M	Runs	Wkts	Best	Ave	5wi
1951	140.2	31	370	15	5-21	24.66	1
1952	208.4	39	647	18	5-87	35.94	1
1953	285	54	859	16	4-52	53.68	
1954	30	8	88	1	1-10	88.00	
1955	131.4	25	446	15	3-22	29.73	
1956	14	2	55	3	3-34	18.33	
1957	10	3	34	0			
1958	54	3	278	9	2-22	30.88	
1959	8	3	16	0			
1960	21	4	83	2	2-25	41.50	
1961	18	5	73	1	1-50	73.00	
1964	3	0	22	0			
Total	**923.4**	**177**	**2971**	**80**	**5-21**	**37.13**	**2**

OVERSEAS

Year	Overs	M	Runs	Wkts	Best	Ave	5wi
1953/54 *(I)*	59.5	11	200	3	1-14	66.66	
1958/59 *(A/NZ)*	2	1	7	0			
1959/60 *(WI)*	53	7	169	4	2-50	42.25	
1961/62 *(I/P)*	2	0	16	0			
1967/68 *(I)*	-						
Total	**116.5**	**19**	**392**	**7**	**2-50**	**56.00**	
Total	**1040.3**	**196**	**3363**	**87**	**5-21**	**38.65**	**2**

BOWLING IN TEST CRICKET

Year	Overs	M	Runs	Wkts
1959/60 *(WI)*	1	0	2	0
Total	**1**	**0**	**2**	**0**

CENTURIES IN FIRST-CLASS CRICKET (30)

For England (3)

100	West Indies	Georgetown	1960
112	Australia	Edgbaston	1961
137	Australia	The Oval	1961

For Cambridge University (2)

100	MCC	Fenner's	1953
146*	Nottinghamshire	Trent Bridge	1953

For Surrey (3)

128	Leicestershire	Loughborough	1953
125	Northants	Northampton	1953
117*	Somerset	The Oval	1954

For Northants (19)

112	Surrey	Guildford	1955
260*	Lancashire	Northampton	1955
102	Worcestershire	Amblecote	1955
132	Nottinghamshire	Trent Bridge	1955
300	Surrey	The Oval	1958
100	Lancashire	Old Trafford	1958
110	Gloucestershire	Northampton	1958
115*	Glamorgan	Ebbw Vale	1958
127*	Derbyshire	Derby	1959
117*	Warwickshire	Northampton	1959
126*	Yorkshire	Headingley	1959
100	Glamorgan	Cardiff	1959
183*	Yorkshire	Northampton	1959
101	Gloucestershire	Bristol	1959
147*	Surrey	The Oval	1960
108	South Africans	Northampton	1960
128	Cambridge University	Northampton	1960
135*	Yorkshire	Northampton	1960
136	Somerset	Taunton	1960

For Combined Services (1)

108	Surrey	The Oval	1956

For Gentlemen (1)

102*	Players	Lord's	1958

For MCC (1)

110	Leeward Islands	Antigua	1960

Acknowledgements and Bibliography

It has been my privilege and pleasure to record for posterity details of Raman Subba Row's long and distinguished career in cricket, first as a player then in administration with Surrey, MCC and the TCCB and as an ICC match referee. My task has been made possible thanks to time freely given for personal visits or on the telephone by countless kind individuals. My heartfelt thanks are due to: Madhav Apte, Peter Arnold, Dr Christopher Barnett, Stephen Chalke, Bernie Coleman, John Cockett, Nick Cook, Michael Cornish, Brian Crump, Alan Davidson, Bob Ely, Gopi Gopinath, Doug Insole, Roger Knight, Peter Lush, Robin Marlar, Derek Newton, Mick Norman, Andrew Radd, Malcolm Scott, Alan Smith, Mike Smith, John Webb and Ossie Wheatley. I am especially grateful to Sir John Major for taking time in a busy life to write a foreword that so perceptively captures the essence of Raman's contribution to the game.

I am grateful for further assistance provided by William Wood, archivist at Whitgift School, and Emma Bennett from the Alumni office at Trinity Hall, Cambridge. At Lord's I received valuable help and guidance from MCC librarian Neil Robinson, and I am particularly grateful to Robert Curphey for scouring the archives for many files pertaining to Raman's involvement with MCC as player and committeeman. At the Oval library Bill Gordon kindly provided access to Surrey yearbooks and other records of Raman's work for the club. My warmest thanks to all.

Special thanks are, of course, due to Raman for long hours patiently spent recalling times long past and to Anne for ensuring that the project never lost momentum and that, whenever I called, my creature comforts were generously taken care of. I am grateful, too, to Alistair Subba Row for many details about the family.

I have made regular use of the following reference books:
Bailey, Thorn & Wynne-Thomas, *Who's Who of Cricketers* (Newnes, 1984)
Christopher Martin-Jenkins, *The Complete Who's Who of Test Cricketers*
                (Macdonald Queen Anne Press, 1987)
Swanton, Plumptre & Woodcock, *Barclays Book of Cricket* (Collins, 1986)
Wisden Cricketers' Almanack
Playfair Cricket Annual
Who's Who
People of Today

For statistics I have relied extensively on CricketArchive. My principal newspaper source has been *The Times*, available on line with the sage words of John Woodcock a constant source of reference.

I have also drawn material and occasionally quoted from:

Madhav Apte, *As Luck would have it* (Global Cricket School, 2015)

Jack Bailey, *Conflicts in Cricket* (The Kingswood Press, 1989)

Jack Bannister & Don Oslear, *Tampering with Cricket* (Collins Willow, 1996)

Scyld Berry, *Cricket Wallah: with England in India 1981-2*
(Hodder & Stoughton, 1982)

Scyld Berry, *A Cricket Odyssey: England on Tour 1987-8* (Pavilion, 1988)

Mihir Bose, *Cricket Voices* (The Kingswood Press, 1990)

Geoffrey Boycott, *The Autobiography* (Guild Publishing, London, 1987)

Stephen Chalke, *At the Heart of English Cricket: the life and memories of Geoffrey Howard* (Fairfield Books, 2001)

Stephen Chalke, *Guess My Story: the life and opinions of Keith Andrew*
(Fairfield Books, 2003)

Stephen Chalke, *Micky Stewart and the changing face of cricket*
(Fairfield Books 2012)

Stephen Chalke, *Summer's Crown: the Story of Cricket's County Championship*
(Fairfield Books, 2015)

George Chesterton & Hubert Doggart, *Oxford and Cambridge Cricket*
(Collins Willow, 1989)

Charles Crawley, *Trinity Hall* (Cambridge, 1976)

Matthew Engel & Andrew Radd, *The History of Northamptonshire Cricket Club*
(Christopher Helm, 1993)

Mike Gatting, *Leading from the Front* (Queen Anne Press, 1988)

Tony Lewis, *Double Century: the Story of MCC and Cricket*
(Hodder & Stoughton, 1987)

Mike Marqusee, *Anyone but England* (Verso, 1994)

Geoffrey Moorhouse, *Lord's* (Hodder & Stoughton, 1983)

Don Mosey, *Boycott* (Guild Publishing, London, 1985)

Peter Oborne, *Wounded Tiger: A history of cricket in Pakistan*
(Simon & Schuster, 2015)

Vasant Raiji, & Anandji Dossa, *CCI & the Brabourne Stadium 1937-1987*
(The CCI Ltd., 1988)

Neil Robinson, *Long Shot Summer: The Year of Four England Captains 1988*
(Amberley Publishing, 2015)

David Sheppard, *Parson's Pitch* (Hodder & Stoughton, 1966)

E.W. Swanton, *Swanton in Australia with MCC 1946 – 1975* (Collins, 1975)

Chris Westcott, *Class of '59: From Bailey to Wooller: The Golden Age of County Cricket* (Mainstream Publishing, 2000)

Charles Williams, *Gentlemen & Players: The Death of Amateurism in Cricket*
(Weidenfeld & Nicholson, 2012)

Graeme Wright, *Betrayal: The Struggle for Cricket's Soul*
(H.F. and G. Witherby, 1993)

I am grateful to the following for giving permission for use of photographs:

Roger Mann   pages 29, 34, 51, 73, 95 and 125
Getty Images   pages 87, 136 and 159
Graham Morris   page 151

In addition I am grateful for the use of photographs supplied by Whitgift School, Surrey County Cricket Club, the Stoics, Mick Norman, Bernie Coleman, Martin Pullon and Mark Rowe. Many of the other photographs have come from the Subba Row family, and some have been taken by myself.

For supply and use of the painting on the front of the book I am grateful to Alistair Subba Row, its owner, and Christina Pierce, the artist.

Finally, throughout the writing of this book, it has been my good fortune to be able to draw on the wise counsel of my friend Stephen Chalke and then to have his meticulous attention to detail and unfailing commitment to high standards in preparing the script for the printers. Errors that readers may find are mine alone.

INDEX

189

INDEX